REMEMBERING LAHAINA

WEST MAUI BOOK SERIES

Series Editor:
LANCE D. COLLINS

The West Maui Book Series, written by local scholars and community leaders, explores and documents the history, culture, and social change of and in West Maui.

Proceedings of the Charter Commissions of the County of Maui
Public Access to the Roads and Trails of West Maui
Kekaʻa: The Making and Saving of North Beach West Maui
The Storied Places of West Maui
Tourism Impacts West Maui
Social Change in West Maui
The Journal of James Macrae: Botanist at the Sandwich Islands, 1825
Lei Nāhonoapiʻilani: Songs of West Maui
Malu ʻUlu o Lele: Maui Komohana in Ka Nupepa Kuokoa
Civil Society in West Maui
Index to the Lahaina News, *the* Lahaina Sun, *and the* Lahaina Times
Water and Power in West Maui
Thinking about Traffic in West Maui
ʻOhuʻohu nā Mauna o ʻEʻeka: Place Names of Maui Komohana
Whose Future?: Community Planning in West Maui
Historical Investigations in West Maui
Reference Guide to the Archaeology of West Maui
Remembering Lahaina

REMEMBERING LAHAINA

What I Learned about Tourism, the ʻĀina and Myself during Twelve Years on Maui

Anthony Pignataro

Lahaina, Maui, Hawaiʻi

© 2025 North Beach-West Maui Benefit Fund, Inc.
All rights reserved
Printed in the United States of America

30 29 28 27 26 25   6 5 4 3 2 1

ISBN 978-1-9524-6112-5 (pbk : alk. paper)

Published by the North Beach-West Maui Benefit Fund, Inc.
P O Box 11329
Lahaina, Hawaiʻi 96761

Distributed by University of Hawaiʻi Press
2840 Kolowalu Street
Honolulu, HI 96822-1888

Every effort has been made to trace copyright holders
and to obtain their permission for the use of copyright material.
The publisher apologizes for any errors or omissions and
would be grateful if notified of any corrections that
should be incorporated in future reprints or editions of this book.

This book is printed on acid-free paper and
meets the guidelines for permanence and durability
of the Council on Library Resources.

Print-ready files provided by North Beach-West Maui Benefit Fund, Inc.

Contents

1. The Fire — 1
2. Olowalu — 9
3. Kahikinui — 13
4. Locals — 18
5. Kiana Davenport — 22
6. Calvin Kuamoʻo — 26
7. Harming the Soul — 30
8. Prison — 35
9. Sugar, Part I — 45
10. Romance of the Skies — 51
11. Kāʻanapali — 63
12. Racism — 70
13. Sewage — 75
14. Eddie Aikau — 78
15. Aloha — 82
16. Sugar, Part II — 90
17. Maui Visitors Bureau — 96
18. Albert Perez — 101
19. Wailea — 105
20. Maui Nō Ka ʻOi — 111
21. Kaleikoa Kaʻeo — 114
22. Age of Stupid — 117

23.	*The White Lotus*	125
24.	"Get a Job"	129
25.	Lahaina and Paradise	137
	Epilogue	143
	Index	145

Chapter 1

THE FIRE

Clyde Wakida adored his house. Located on Puapihi Street in the southern end of Lahaina Town, the house was ornate without being ostentatious, and surrounded by lush tropical plants and palm trees. It was luxurious, but still easy to relax in. Set just a few lots back from the ocean, the house was a short walk from the town's public tennis courts, which were named after Shigeto "Shigesh" Wakida, Clyde's father. Clyde played tennis too, but had made a career in construction. He'd built the house on Puapihi Street, designing and placing everything, including the molding, himself. The house, Clyde's daughter Alexa Hanohano recalled, was her father's "most prized possession."

In the late afternoon of August 8, 2023, a wildfire tore through Lahaina Town. Fanned by 60-mile-an-hour force winds from Hurricane Dora, what had been a smoldering fire an hour before suddenly exploded into a firestorm, blowing embers across town in minutes. It was a Tuesday, and Clyde, his wife Penny and their dog were home. As thick black smoke filled their neighborhood, they decided that Penny would take the dog and leave, while Clyde would follow behind. Penny escaped, but soon realized that Clyde wasn't behind her. Alexa, their daughter, later surmised that Clyde stayed behind to protect their house.

County officials wouldn't know the full extent of the damage done to Lahaina until the next morning. But one resident who lived through the fire, Kekoa Lansford, knew the horrors the fire had caused. Since Tuesday night, he'd been helping rescue people who found themselves trapped and had waded into the ocean. Many had survived all night this way—staying in the shallows until they got too cold, then venturing onto shore until the heat drove them back into the water—but some had not.

The next morning, Chelsea Davis, a Honolulu TV news reporter who'd grown up on Maui, made her way into what was left of the town. She came across Lansford near the Lahaina Jodo Mission, home of one of the largest Buddha statues outside the Japanese home islands—one of many cultural treasures of Lahaina lost in the fire. There, Lansford told Davis of what had happened during the night, and how he couldn't save everyone. "We still got dead bodies in the water, floating, and on the sea wall," Lansford told Davis on camera in a report that aired soon after. "They've been sitting there since last night."

About the same time, a friend of the Wakidas' made his way to their house. Penny hadn't heard from Clyde all night, and was deeply worried. That morning, thousands of Lahaina residents were unaccounted for, and since there was no power in town, and local cellphone towers had been damaged or destroyed, it was possible Clyde was still alive somewhere. But when Penny's friend saw Clyde's burned-out truck still parked in their driveway, she feared the worst.

Three months after the fire, those driving by Lahaina could still smell ash and burnt flesh, but county officials were still finalizing the exact death toll. Because so many bodies were badly burned, the best officials could do was provide an estimate that 100 people died—fairly close to the final toll. In many cases, the coroner's office had to use DNA samples to confirm identities.

On August 22, exactly two weeks after the fire, the Maui Police Department announced that Clyde Wakida was dead. He was 74.

I knew Clyde. I'd lived on the island for a dozen years, working as a newspaper editor and reporter. His wife, Penny, had worked with my girlfriend Angie on a Lahaina theater nonprofit for children, and Angie often visited their house on Puapihi Street to get information or documents signed. Clyde was a gentle person with friendly eyes and a relaxed smile. In early November, his family held a celebration of life ceremony for him at Launiupoko, a beach park a couple minutes south of Lahaina that's long been popular with local residents. A couple hundred people showed up to listen to music, talk story about Clyde's life, and cry.

With just a couple exceptions, all who perished in the fire were Lahaina residents. The youngest confirmed death was a seven-year-old boy; the oldest a 97-year-old woman. Older people accounted for most of the dead, with more than 70 percent of those who died over the age of 60.

Filipino people, who often work service industry jobs on Maui, also made up a large portion of the dead, according to Steven West, an agent with the ILWU who represents many Lahaina workers. One Filipino family lost nine members, ranging in age from 30 to 77, though the remains of one woman, Lydia Coloma, were never located.

Compounding the tragedy was the loss of more than 2,200 structures. County officials estimated that 86 percent of the buildings damaged or destroyed in the blaze were residential. Within a month of the fire, more than 7,000 residents were in shelters, first in gyms and later in hotels that had been emptied of tourists in the first hours after the fire. The majority were traumatized and grieving, having lost friends, relatives, pets, homes that had been in their families for generations, possessions, and in many cases, their jobs, businesses, and livelihoods.

In all, the Lahaina Fire was the worst American wildfire in over a century.

Many were also angry. "People are pissed, and it's justifiable," Autumn Ness, a staffer for the nine-member Maui County Council, told the panel two weeks after the fire. Ness described a "collective rage" that took hold of the community immediately after the blaze, fanned by years of warnings that wildfire risk threatened much of inhabited Maui—warnings that seemingly went unheeded.

Sergio Alcubilla is the co-executive director of the Hawai'i Workers Center, which advocates for low-wage workers across the state, many of whom are undocumented. Nearly a month after the fire, on August 27, he articulated the anger Ness spoke of perfectly at a rally held at the state capitol in Honolulu. His comments deserve to be quoted at some length:

> Lahaina's fate is really the fate of every working family here in Hawai'i. Our state has been failing at working-class families for decades, because it has consistently put the interests of visitors and outside corporations ahead of its very own people. It's heartbreaking to see our state leaders doubling down on this mindset as they continue to facilitate the exploitation of these islands . . . We are not expendable. Our resources are not expendable. My people are not expendable. As we rebuild, we rebuild together the right way. We must put people over profits.

Maui's hotels were outstanding sources of short-term housing, but Ness and Alcubilla were warning that thousands of Lahaina residents were still on the edge of survival—they had no time to rest and recover and grieve because they were too busy filling out emergency aid and housing applications. Most weren't working and had no idea when they would be able to return to work. Some who were scared, overwhelmed, or simply exhausted left Maui altogether for the continental United States—when, or even if, they would return, no one could say.

But those who remained knew the instant they got their hotel room, a clock began ticking. They knew it because many of those displaced by the fire were themselves service industry workers. They knew better than most how the hotels were the backbone of the island's economy, and if the resorts couldn't make money, everyone on the island, and maybe even the state, was in trouble.

Christine Borge was one of them. A service industry worker prior to the fire, Borge had lost her house on Wainee Street and everything in it except her dog. She was sheltering at the Royal Lahaina Resort when the Maui County Council heard public testimony on August 22. "Who is benefitting" from all the paperwork she was having to fill out, she asked the councilmembers with some bitterness, before telling them that it was a mistake to tell tourists not to go to Maui. "Maui needs tourists now," Borge said.

State officials were scared, too. Though West Maui had been closed to tourists immediately after the fire, everyone knew their return was inevitable. Seventy cents of every dollar in Maui's economy directly or indirectly came from tourism—an astonishingly high percentage. Officials from Governor Josh Green to President Joe Biden promised that the recovery and rebuilding of Lahaina would take place at the pace dictated by residents, but that proved true only to a point. Exactly one month after the fire, Green announced that West Maui hotels would reopen for business the very next month, on October 8.

The reason was simple, James Tokioka, director of the state's Department of Business, Economic Development and Tourism, told Maui County Councilmembers a few days after Green's announcement. "People are hurting; we know that," Tokioka said. But he added that "hotels were going to lay off their employees after October 1" if state officials kept the West Maui restriction in place. Fearing further economic catastrophe, and knowing that the multinational corporations that owned Maui's largest resorts weren't bluffing, state officials agreed to let the tourists return.

But many residents felt it was just too soon. "There's FEMA signs; there's still Red Cross signs," Albert Perez, executive director of the community non-profit Maui Tomorrow, told *The Guardian*. "It all just seems premature."

Though Green later said that no one would be evicted from their shelter to make way for tourists, more than 3,000 Lahaina residents—nearly half the entire town—signed a petition asking state and county officials to hold off returning tourists to West Maui. For them, the thought of people who'd just eight weeks prior lost their homes, pets or even family members having to serve Mai Tais and fish tacos to people enjoying their vacation proved too awful to contemplate. While Green said he sympathized with their case, the best residents got was a "phased" approach in which the high-end resorts in Kapalua, located furthest away from the burn zone, opened first, with the resorts of Kāʻanapali following not quite a month later. Even when Green added that those residents who weren't ready to go back to work could take the time they needed, he still appealed to their sense of duty and guilt, basically telling them that the whole island was depending on them.

"[T]hink of your neighbor, or think of the business next to you," Green said in early October, according to the Associated Press. "Or think of the impact of having only, say, 40 percent of the travelers that we normally have to Maui."

For Maui Tomorrow's Perez, this was the COVID-19 pandemic all over again. "Every time they build another hotel room, the community becomes a little more dependent on these jobs, and then when that industry takes a hit, which it regularly does, we end up with an even worse economic crisis," he told *The Guardian*.

Like the COVID-19 pandemic, the Lahaina wildfire hurt nearly everyone on Maui. Though the devastation was largely confined to Lahaina (though 19 homes were destroyed in Upcountry Maui the same day as Lahaina during a separate blaze), businesses all over Maui were suffering.

Les Tomita was one of many. Born on Oʻahu, Tomita had opened Da Kitchen in 1998. His little restaurants in Kahului and later Kihei quickly became legendary for serving oversized plate lunches—heaping mounds of chicken katsu, chili, loco moco or other staples, all served with two fist-sized scoops of sticky white rice and another scoop of potato-mac salad. Soon national food and travel media noticed, and before he knew it, Casey Webb was cracking wise in his Kahului location for an episode of the Travel Channel's popular series *Man v. Food*. Once the envy of other local restaurants for its immense popularity with tourists—70 percent of his customers were visitors, Tomita told the Maui County Council in mid-September—business at Da Kitchen all but collapsed after the fire, even though he had no locations in West Maui.

"The smart guys closed," Tomita told councilmembers, choking up repeatedly. "But I'm choosing to stay open. I have single mothers who can't pay their rent. My job is to be the correct citizen of Maui."

Farms, too, were in bad shape. In fact, about 50 farms on the island had been impacted by the August 8 fires—mostly from the high winds from Hurricane Dora that had fanned initial blazes into deadly infernos, according to Koa Hewahewa, deputy director of the county's Department of Agriculture.

"Everyone will feel the effects," Hewahewa told councilmembers. "We're crying for help."

Compounding the problem was the fact that many island farmers depended on West Maui restaurants to buy their produce—a product of a years-long effort to get resorts and restaurants to highlight locally grown fruits, vegetables and meat. Now, with so many restaurants gone, and those that remained largely empty, farmers were growing desperate.

Though officials said determining the exact cause of the fire would take a year or more, it was immediately clear that the conditions around the island that made such a blaze possible had been more than a century in the making. I wasn't surprised when wildfire experts told the Maui County Council in mid-September that society's relationship with the land was "broken," because I'd seen more than enough evidence of that in my dozen years spent writing and reporting on Maui.

For that time, I was editor of the alternative newsweekly *MauiTime*. It was a tiny, eternally underfunded and mismanaged paper, but I loved every minute of my time there. The staff was tiny, so the job required me not just to oversee all stories each week, but also to be the chief news reporter, investigator and copy editor. Each week I discussed the cover image with the art director, assigned stories to freelancers, edited entertainment briefs (called "picks of the week") for the calendar section, wrote a news column and reported news that I felt the other news organizations on Maui were missing. The work put me in contact with remarkable people, but it also quickly taught me that the island that hundreds of thousands of tourists were seeing every year was profoundly different than the one residents—especially those of Native Hawaiian (Kanaka) descent—lived on. Yes, crime and drugs were certainly issues, but the focus of county government, at least when I first moved there in 2003, seemed more focused on land developers and big resorts than residents. And while nearly three quarters of the economy depended on tourism, for the most part, the jobs local people were working didn't provide anything like a standard of living required to live comfortably. As the years went by and property values skyrocketed, homeownership for residents became increasingly difficult, if not outright impossible.

I left the island, and *MauiTime,* for good in 2018. My girlfriend, Angie, and I could no longer afford to live there. Though both of us were college educated and had professional jobs in the continental United States, neither of us could ever find anything like the salary our education and experience deserved. My salary as editor had frozen in 2010 or so at the grand sum of $42,000 a year, and it was clear to me that though I did my job well, a raise was never going to happen. Though we both missed Maui, we stayed in touch with friends. On August 8, 2023, I was vaguely aware of fires around the island, but they seemed no different than those we often dealt with during the summer months when we lived there. Once, a wildfire on the Pali (the sea cliff between Māʻalaea and Ukumehame) had flared up while Angie was working in Kāʻanapali, forcing her to spend the night there with a nice tourist who offered to help her out.

But when I awoke early on August 9, I started to see the word "destroyed" in Instagram posts about Lahaina. When Angie got up, we found the Hawaii News Now app on our Apple TV and started streaming the live news broadcast. For the next few days, all we watched was local Hawaiʻi news about a fire that had, in fact, destroyed a town both of us had worked in and loved. My first office had been in a small office and retail complex called 505 Front Street, located near the southern end of town. In later years, Angie maintained a small office in that same building when she worked as a part-time executive director for the small Lahaina theater nonprofit for kids. The fire had obliterated it, we soon saw, as aerial images of the burn zone began to circulate in the news and on social media. The next day, I got a call from the head of *Maui Times,* a monthly magazine that formed after my old alt-weekly *MauiTime* had shut down during the COVID-19 pandemic. He and I had worked together at *MauiTime,* and now he wanted news coverage of the fire's aftermath. Since I wasn't doing much newswriting at the time, I agreed, and spent the next couple of months reporting remotely from my home in Long Beach, California, on how Maui was dealing with the fire and what the future lay in store, as far as I could tell. Though I worked nonstop for weeks and wrote dozens of stories, the loss of business from the fire proved too much, and *Maui Times* went out of business at the end of September.

The causes of the fires that burned so much of Maui are the subject of numerous investigations by a variety of government agencies, none of which are anywhere near complete as I write this. But I still wanted to write something on how Maui had gotten to the point where even in the midst of a historic and deadly tragedy, the governor felt the need to shame residents into going back to their jobs serving tourists. This, I knew very well. Maui is a deceptively complex place—full of beauty and wonder, certainly, but also unforgiving if you choose not to work in the service industry. As such, this is not a typical memoir. Rather, think of it as a chronicle of what I learned about Maui while working there as a journalist. Many of the essays and dispatches collected here deal with island history, as well as places and people seldom glimpsed by visitors. They're mostly in chronological order, but the learning process rarely happens in a strictly linear fashion. Some of the stories are humorous, others grim. But throughout it all, I tried to include the evolution of my own thinking. Though left-wing when I first arrived on island in August 2003, I still looked at the world much like most straight white American men. Race and gender simply weren't part of my internal calculations, and I certainly didn't think of myself as an interloper. But the more I interacted with Maui, got to know its people and problems, the more I realized my traditional thought processes were insufficient, if not actually harmful. My work and presence on Maui changed me—I'd like to think for the better, but it was never an easy progression. Even now, as the island takes its first steps to dealing with trauma that will last decades, if not generations, I wonder whether it's my place to say anything at all about my experiences there. Ultimately, I agreed to do so simply because there is material in the work I did as a reporter that I haven't seen anywhere else—information vital to anyone who wants to understand why such a devastating fire could happen at a place so many people consider paradise.

Chapter 2

OLOWALU

Almost exactly two decades prior to the Lahaina fire, I was sitting in a folding chair under a huge monkeypod tree at the old Plantation Manager's House in Olowalu, located on the coast a few minutes south of Lahaina. People often get married at the house, and the landing out front later appeared a few times in the first season of the HBO series *The White Lotus*. I could hear the surf break on the shoreline rocks maybe 50 yards away. There were a few dozen chairs, most of them filled with white people like me, on the emerald-green lawn. The only difference between them and me is that I wasn't supposed to be there.

It was late October 2003, and I'd been on Maui barely two months. I knew my way around the island and was in the midst of reading the fantastic 1990 book *Land and Power in Hawaii,* about the connections between politics, organized crime and land development, which would influence me throughout my career on island, but I was still really "fresh off the boat," as locals would say. I was undercover, infiltrating a coaching session for upwardly mobile West Maui residents set up by four land owners and developers. They were pushing for a controversial housing development known as "Puʻunoa," just a couple miles away on land dedicated to agriculture at the southern end of Lahaina Town (though most land developers on Maui are white, project names always carry Hawaiian names, which is typically done for public relations reasons). Sold as a way to bring much-needed affordable homes to West Maui, county officials actually hated the project because it would add pressure to Lahaina's already strained roads and infrastructure, as well as mess up plans to build a future bypass road into town. Despite county officials, including the mayor, repeatedly pointing out that the project would never bring in nearly as many affordable homes as was promised, the project's developers succeeded in convincing state officials to fast-track the deal. But a key County Council vote was looming, and those pushing the project wanted a long line of residents to talk up the project's benefits at the council meeting.

Somehow, my publisher got wind of the late afternoon coaching session, so I grabbed my notepad and headed out. It was a sweet journalistic scoop. Peter Martin and Jim Riley, the owners of West Maui Land Company, which owns thousands of acres from the Pali tunnel to Lahaina Town, were there. Michele McLean, one of their agents whom I would encounter years later under very different circumstances, was there, too. Since the 1990s, "almost every conversation about land in West Maui, and especially in Lahaina and the surrounding areas, begins and ends with the mention of these individuals and their companies," the Hawaiian historian and political scientist Sydney Iaukea has written. Another developer, Jim Whitehead, who had spent much of the session drinking cans of Budweiser from a cooler placed at his feet, noted that because women were in the group, he couldn't "tell some stories" about the mayor and a particularly vocal councilmember. When a woman who clearly supported the project asked when developers would stop converting old agricultural lands into housing, developer Kent Smith, who had actually assaulted an activist a couple years prior, shook his head. "Growth is inevitable," he told the crowd, virtually all of which nodded in agreement. "Growth is inevitable. Growth is inevitable." Though I was sitting in the middle of the group furiously taking notes about all this, no one asked who I was or what I was doing—most likely because I was white like everyone else.

I still think about that visit to Olowalu, though not because of the housing project that necessitated it (which was never built). Even then, I knew Olowalu was more than just a general store, wedding venue and juice stand. Many tourists who visit Maui know about Olowalu, which sits on the Honoapi'ilani Highway just south of Lahaina, but only as a place they pass through as they head to and from their Kā'anapali resorts. A few know about the large number of ancient petroglyphs in the area, but little else. "The Lehua tree and blossom once filled the forests in Olowalu and turned the streams red with their petals," according to historian Sydney Iaukea. Though much drier today because of water diversions caused by the old Pioneer sugar mill in the 1800s, trees still hang over the ocean and shelter one of the last healthy coral reefs in the state. But Olowalu also has a dark, violent past—one few tourists or even transplants really know.

Olowalu was once home to a large and thriving Kanaka Maoli village. The land was lush with taro and sweet potato patches. But in 1790, at about the spot where I was seated on a folding chair jotting down the mutterings and ramblings of land developers, an American sea captain named Simon Metcalfe anchored his brig just off shore, then opened fire on what had been a large Hawaiian settlement, killing more than a hundred men, women and children and wounding 150 more. "Many families had brought their children for the day's outing to see the foreign ship," historian Aubrey Janion wrote. "They came in good faith, trusting in the word of the ship's commander that they would not be harmed." Metcalfe was taking revenge for the death of one of his sailors, and his method was overwhelming, barbaric, and absolutely in line with how Americans have historically dealt with indigenous peoples who refused to kneel.

Clifford Naeole works as a cultural adviser for the Ritz-Carlton in Kapalua, a spectacular region of West Maui known for lavish hotels, golf courses and a massive burial of more than a thousand Kanaka remains dating back centuries, the discovery of which in the 1980s eventually forced construction of the resort away from the coast and set the stage for the modern protection of Native Hawaiian remains. Many of the major resorts employ individuals like Naeole to offer Kanaka perspective on matters like hotel construction (when the Ritz-Carlton Maui opened a new "Aloha Garden Pavilion" that is patterned after Hawaiian voyaging canoes in November 2023, the hotel GM told reporters that it couldn't have been done without Naeole's support and assistance). But Naeole is also an expert in Kanaka history and traditions, and knows all about what happened at Olowalu. He's driven past Olowalu for more than two decades as he heads to and from work. He often thinks about the massacre that took place there, which he calls "Hawaiʻi's Wounded Knee."

"You tend to think about things when you're driving," he told me in 2016. "I knew that something there was wrong. There's an energy there that's never been cleared, never been released."

Maui has an enormously complex history and political culture that most tourists—and transplants—know nothing about. When I first moved to Maui, I'd never heard the term "settler colonialism" before, but I eventually learned it well. Hawaiʻi isn't a state like Delaware or Missouri, or even California—it's a true colony, closer to Guam and Puerto Rico.

Its culture and traditions were trampled by American occupation and rule, sure, but they were also glamorized, sexualized, and above all, commercialized. Smith's mantra that "growth is inevitable" is entirely American, and has no meaning for pre-contact Kanaka people. They not only had their land stolen from them, but generations later now have to endure seeing white people get rich by selling bastardized versions of their own culture and traditions to tourists at luaus—which have degenerated into dinner shows with musicians singing "Tiny Bubbles" while sunburned visitors scoop kālua pork out of a giant buffet bowl and chat about not seeing enough turtles during their snorkel trip. Of course, all this is still going on, in the form of buying and selling land taken hundreds of years ago from the Hawaiian people without proper compensation or even negotiation. Big, expensive homes are still being built throughout West Maui, as well as large sea walls and hardened shorelines (climate change and sea level rise have been steadily devouring Maui's coastline for decades) and are often planned for Olowalu itself, though resident activism has largely been successful in stopping, or at least minimizing, growth there. The seawalls, at least those that have been built, often damage offshore reefs but do little to stop encroaching waves from splashing onto the highway that runs from Lahaina to the Pali. "Olowalu is special," Hawaiian practitioner Naeole told me. "Olowalu is a place with significance. But Olowalu as a place is not really recognized. It needs to have its own sense of place. There needs to be an altar, a temple, erected there, just like Wounded Knee." Though Naeole has huge stature on Maui, and is well known and respected within the powerful tourist industry itself, such a temple, or just a marker, remains unbuilt in Olowalu.

In 2019, Iaukea asked me for a quote on Olowalu for an essay she was writing. "Will there ever be a time when Americans stop damaging Olowalu in the name of greed, ignorance, and racism?" I told her. "Seawalls and subdivisions spring from the same hubris we've seen since Metcalf's massacre: the United States will reshape Olowalu (and Maui, and Hawai'i) regardless of what those who were there first have to say."

But I missed something when I made that statement: locals often damage Olowalu, too. Decades of plans to develop Olowalu were one thing, but in January 2024, the Maui County Council approved a proposal to bury debris from Lahaina Town in Olowalu, rather than ship it off-island. The burial was to be "temporary," according to the Council, though exactly how long the debris would remain there is impossible to say. Though a great many residents spoke out against the plan before the Council, the vote to approve was overwhelming. Given that the debris most likely contains both toxic elements and human remains, Olowalu will remain a place of tragedy and death for years to come.

Chapter 3

KAHIKINUI

My official job title at *Maui Time* was editor, which required me to assign and track stories as well as consult with the art director on each week's cover image, but the paper was so small I also worked as copy editor and chief reporter. I had exactly one full-time staffer—an associate editor position held by an extremely talented but still inexperienced writer named Samantha Campos (today she's editor of *East Bay Magazine* in Oakland, California). In the days when social media was still in its infancy, Sam and I wrote thousands of words each week, but readers didn't see them—either in print or online—until each Thursday when we went to press. I wrote a lot back then, but I also had to interview a wide variety of people about a huge array of subjects, which got me up to speed on Maui politics very quickly. I filed some of the paper's first public records requests. One, for the police reports on a resident who'd died while being arrested, was very heavily redacted. County policy was to blot out the names of all police officers in the otherwise public reports, and I feared I wouldn't be able to put together a narrative of what had happened, until I realized that someone at the county attorney's office had (either accidentally or on purpose) failed to redact each of the involved officers' names at some point in the report. Doing so allowed me to figure out who was who, making it possible to explain to readers exactly how the arrest had gone bad.

I worked pretty much every day my first month on Maui. To relax, I ventured away from the office when things were quiet, not looking for activities like the majority of Maui visitors, but alone time. Though there are plenty of places on Maui to get away from tourists (or people in general), I quickly found that my favorite was Kahikinui. One of the most important spots on Maui, it's also the most desolate, and it's always been like that. Archaeologists generally believe that the first Polynesians to arrive in Hawai'i landed at Kahikinui, on Maui's southeastern coast, about a thousand years ago. The name roughly translates as "Big Tahiti," and the area clearly held immense wayfinding importance to pre-contact Hawaiians. But the region is rocky and foreboding; from the Pi'ilani Highway, the only paved (more or less) road that traverses the area, the ocean seems metallic and far off. I would drive through there, maybe even stop at a bend in the road near the coast, and just take in the jagged coastline and steel gray ocean. But most of the access through the area is limited, which is perfectly fine by me. Beyond some Hawaiians, few live there today, which is pretty much as it's always been.

Archaeologist Patrick Vinton Kirch knows the area better than anyone. He'd been studying the region for 17 years when his book, *Kua'āina Kahiko,* was published. He calls Kahikinui Maui's "most remote and undeveloped region" and a "classic *kua'āina,* a backcountry that was shunned by the ruling chiefs." It was so isolated, Kirch says, that there were "no rich *mo'olelo,* oral traditions, about Kahikinui." Instead, the "district was populated largely by *maka'āinana,* common folk, who were derided by officials of the nineteenth-century Hawaiian Kingdom as *'ili ulaula,* 'red skins,' a reference to their sunburned bodies, reflecting long hours of toil in the sweet potato patches."

But for archaeological research, Kahikinui holds thousands of archaeological sites, precisely because westerners (and most Hawaiians) had largely ignored the region. "First and foremost, Kahikinui constituted an entire *moku,* an ancient political district, which had never suffered from the effects of Westernized 'development,'" Kirch wrote in his book. "Precisely because it is a backwater, lacking in freshwater or rich soils, Kahikinui was spared the effects of sugarcane or pineapple plantations." For Kirch, this meant that the layout of the original inhabitants' homes, agricultural fields, heiau, and other structures would still largely be intact. "I could think of few other places in the islands where an entire region could be studied on such a scale," he wrote.

Kirch's work in Kahikinui also put him in touch with Kanaka activists, who formed Ka 'Ohana o Kahikinui in the early 1980s. "Being able to watch as they fought to gain access to Hawaiian lands, and in a few small ways to aid them in their quest, lent additional meaning to my research," Kirch wrote. "It brought our goal of understanding the ancient history of this land into direct contact with the continuing efforts of the Hawaiian people to preserve and perpetuate their culture."

Kirch's studied reverence for Hawaiian culture and artifacts is sadly rare in post-contact history. In fact, Americans have rarely done well for the Hawaiian

Islands. The first westerners brought disease and military technology that quickly wreaked havoc on the Kānaka Maoli. The Kānaka numbered about 683,000 in 1778, when Captain James Cook first dropped anchor off Hawai'i Island. But he brought disease with him—germs the local population had no defense against. According to UC Riverside researcher David Swanson, Kānaka began to die immediately thereafter.

Swanson estimated that one in 17 Native Hawaiians died within two years of Cook's arrival, according to a Pew Research Center report from 2015. That was an extremely high death rate, but it was nothing compared to what was coming. By the year 1800, the Kanaka population had declined nearly 50 percent. A generation later, in 1820, the population had declined 71 percent. By 1840, an astonishing 84 percent of the Kanaka population was gone. That's eight of 10 people wiped out in a 60-year time frame. Were the same thing to happen to the United States in, say, 1960, when the population was about 180 million people, there would be just 28.8 million Americans left in 2020—about the population of Venezuela today.

This is genocide, and Hawai'i never recovered. What society could? Such deaths left the islands exposed to westerners who could come in and commercialize, and militarize, as they saw fit. When Cook landed, Ford Island in Pearl Harbor—known to Kānaka as Moku'ume'ume—was a place where married couples who found difficulty having children could go during the Makahiki Festival to, well, help speed things along. By the early twentieth century, the U.S. Army, and later the Navy, maintained a fighter airfield there (the sex rituals having been banned decades ago by missionaries).

By this point, everything in Hawai'i was up for grabs, but initially it was the land that made white Americans rich. For the Kānaka Maoli, the land was more than simply sacred. It was a family member—to be respected above all. This was their concept of kuleana—the need for everyone to be responsible for the good of the land, and in turn, the land would provide in the form of food, clothing, and shelter. There could be no private property in such a society; instead, Kānaka used the land use concept of ahupua'a, in which all islands were divided into parcels that started in the mountains and stretched to the shore, giving everyone equal access to all the natural resources Hawai'i offered.

Of course, that all changed after the Americans moved in. They needed hundreds of thousands of acres for their highly industrialized sugar and pineapple plantations. Of course, neither crop was indigenous to Hawai'i, though the earliest Polynesians who arrived did bring some cane with them. The industrialized plantation—staffed with workers from Portugal, Puerto Rico, the

Philippines, Japan, and China because so few Kānaka were left—was an entirely Western innovation.

The so-called "Great Māhele" of 1848, when King Kamehameha III introduced private land ownership and Western methods of land surveying, was especially destructive to the local culture. For non-royalty, the concept of private property was completely alien, and led directly to the Hawaiian people's loss of control over their own land. "This unfamiliarity, coupled with numerous legal and logistical constraints, led to foreign acquisition of large amounts of land intended for Native Hawaiians," stated the 2012 Maui General Plan introduction. "Many Hawaiian families were required to leave the lands they had cultivated for generations and were forced to move to populated towns such as Wailuku and Lahaina."

The disenfranchisement of the Hawaiian people was cruel and deliberate. The "Bayonet Constitution," imposed on the monarchy in 1887 by the sugar barons, required that those running—or even just voting—for the House of Nobles hold at least $3,000 in assets or $600 in annual income. Right there, two-thirds of what remained of Native Hawaiians had no say in the governing of their own land. When Liliʻuokalani assumed the throne following the death of her brother Kalākaua, she began to take steps to dismantle the Bayonet Constitution. But she was never able to finish the job.

On January 17, 1893, the American elite—assisted by 160 members of the U.S. military—toppled the queen in a bloodless but blatantly illegal coup, imprisoning her in ʻIolani Palace. Though then-President Grover Cleveland opposed the coup and refused to recognize the new "Hawaiian Republic"—of which only whites were actual citizens—his successor William McKinley had no such qualms. In fact, he went one step further and ordered the complete takeover of Hawaiʻi at the close of the Spanish–American War in 1898.

The queen—seen by many Kānaka today as the last legitimate political leader of Hawaiʻi—understood perfectly the character of the men who'd stolen her kingdom. They're still in the US, bloated with entitlement but still hungry for more power, regardless of the damage inflicted on others. Indeed, it is impossible not to think of Trump and the January 6 insurrectionists after reading the queen's words.

"It has been shown that in Hawaiʻi there is an alien element composed of men of energy and determination, well able to carry through what they undertake, but not scrupulous respecting their methods," Liliʻuokalani wrote in her memoir *Hawaii's Story by Hawaii's Queen*. "They doubtless control all the resources and influence of the present ruling power in Honolulu, and will employ them tirelessly in the future, as they have in the past, to secure their ends. This annexationist party might prove to be a dangerous accession even to American politics, both on account of natural abilities, and because of the training of an autocratic life from earliest youth."

Incredibly, the U.S. government officially apologized for all this. In November 1993, President Bill Clinton signed Public Law 103–150, known as the "Apology Resolution." Introduced by U.S. Senator Daniel Akaka (who was Hawaiian) on the 100th anniversary of the overthrow of Liliʻuokalani, the resolution stated that "the overthrow of the Kingdom of Hawaiʻi occurred with the active participation of agents and citizens of the United States and further acknowledges that the Native Hawaiian people never directly relinquished to the United States their claims to their inherent sovereignty as a people over their national lands, either through the Kingdom of Hawaiʻi or through a plebiscite or referendum." But the resolution is just an apology—nothing physically or legally changed regarding Hawaiʻi following its adoption. In fact, though it was passed by both houses of Congress and signed by the president, the resolution actually carries "no binding legal effect," according to the U.S. Supreme Court. The end result is that the U.S. government collectively shrugged its shoulders, mouthed "my bad," and then went about its business, which is probably the most American thing that the government could do.

* * *

The lack of true restorative justice in Hawaiʻi harms the islands to this day. The activist Mariame Kaba says there are three assumptions underlying true restorative justice:

> The harming of people and relationships creates needs;
> These needs lead to obligations;
> The obligation is to "put right" whatever has been harmed.

In Hawaiʻi, nothing about the original coup that obliterated the Hawaiian Kingdom has been put right. Certainly, anyone in Hawaiʻi can participate in the American system of government, but for those who refuse to acknowledge the legality of that system, they have no recourse. While many of Kanaka descent choose to work within the American structure, and do so quite well, I saw a growing unease throughout Hawaiʻi during my time on Maui. The construction of massive telescopes on Hawaiʻi Island and Maui became major flashpoints that remain rallying cries for indigenous sovereignty.

Chapter 4

LOCALS

There's a lot of anger on Maui, as I learned repeatedly throughout my time as editor. Not that every grievance from someone locally born leads back to the imprisonment of Liliʻuokalani, but generational trauma like that, unanswered for a century, has a tendency to bleed into just about every aspect of life. The energy, profoundly negative as it is, has to go somewhere.

It doesn't help that, unless you're one of the few who make it to a top management position, life on Maui for most workers is pretty rough. Because Maui is a remote island, the cost of living is high. And because the service industry occupies so much of the local economy, wages are generally low. Do the math—I'm still amazed we lasted so long, given that most of the other white transplants I've known barely lasted a year before returning to the Lower 48.

At various times, my girlfriend Angie worked selling trinkets (mostly bongs) to tourists at an open-air market, managing the office of a struggling photographer, working as a hotel concierge, serving as executive director of a small nonprofit that provided theater camp for West Maui kids, doing marketing for a South Maui real estate company, and supervising a pool slide at a popular Kāʻanapali resort. That job was the worst. All day, she would sit in the blazing sun and tell unruly kids (and their often more unruly parents) when it was safe for them to go down the slide. "You have the best job in the world," people would tell her as she wiped sweat off her brow, as though merely sitting atop a fake rock and getting to look at the ocean was the pinnacle of human achievement. Then came the questions—the stupid, stupid questions.

"Do you live on Maui?"

—Amazingly enough, yes.

"What's that building out there?"
—You mean the cruise ship?
"Does Maui take American money?"

Look, I know going on vacation can be a bewildering experience. But at some point, mere ignorance gives way to a pernicious sense of entitlement. Someone who understands that better than most is Sydney Iaukea. These days, she holds a doctorate in political science and writes books about Hawaiian history and land development. But when she was younger, growing up on Maui, Iaukea worked in the big Kāʻanapali resorts (she even won the title of Miss Lahaina in a beauty pageant). Like all employees, she found herself schooled in the art of catering to tourists—even to the point of taking classes in how to show adequate "aloha" for guests.

"I was deeply disturbed by these experiences, but not able to adequately formalize or articulate the problem," Iaukea wrote in her 2014 book *Kekaʻa: The Making and Saving of North Beach West Maui*. "It would be many years before I could put into words the discomfort I felt for being treated like a servant, and told to do so with a smile on my face and aloha in my heart. I have been critical of the tourism industry ever since."

Reading Iaukea's book was like getting handed a tall glass of water after walking across a lava field. Here was a clear explanation of how out of balance Hawaiʻi's economy had become—and how much damage that did to both the land (what Kānaka called the ʻāina) and the indigenous culture in the process. Remember that 70 cents out of every dollar in Maui's economy is in some way connected to the tourist industry. In practical terms, this means that when the big hotels want something—land for expansion, restricted public beach access, etc.—they get it.

"Following closely behind sugar production, the hotel developers did not need to invent a new social narrative of this land, but simply build on the narrative of theft already enacted by the sugar growers—one that viewed the ʻāina as empty space," Iaukea wrote. "Getting off the plantation is easier to imagine than accomplish, because it takes a paradigm shift regarding the purpose of the land and people and industry . . . For many years, local history and livelihoods have reflected the economic rhetoric of two industries—sugar and tourism—and tourism still has a stranglehold on government and individual perceptions of growth and opportunity."

Ever since the toppling of Liliʻuokalani's government, Kānaka Maoli have watched their culture and language appropriated for commercial purposes beyond their control. This is the hubris of settler colonialism—people come in, then feel entitled to just take what they want.

This was readily apparent throughout the twentieth century and into the 21st, when Hawaiian Commercial & Sugar (HC&S)—a subsidiary of Alexander & Baldwin (A&B) and the last sugar plantation in Hawai'i—diverted public water away from East Maui for its sugar fields. Hawaiian taro farmers and activists fought for decades to restore the water, but the State of Hawai'i let it go on. And on. Even after HC&S closed in 2016, A&B still fought in the courts to keep the water—water that never belonged to the company in the first place. "Our kūpuna from East Maui, they testified and they got hurt and they're exhausted," Mary Ann Pahukoa, an East Maui taro farmer, told KITV News in Honolulu in early 2016. "They're tired and emotionally, it's a burden. We're exhausted too, but we understand that it's our kuleana as the next generation to take on this fight."

You saw this in early 2017, when Facebook boss Mark Zuckerberg—one of the richest men in the world—began filing quiet title lawsuits against hundreds of Hawaiians who lived near his 700-acre estate on Kaua'i. The suits are used to clear up land title issues, but in the case of Hawai'i, where all land was essentially stolen in the late nineteenth century (or even earlier), such suits do little more than stoke already considerable anger among those who can trace their heritage in Hawai'i back centuries. "This is the face of neocolonialism," University of Hawai'i law professor Kapua Sproat told *The Guardian* at the time. "Even though a forced sale may not physically displace people, it's the last nail in the coffin of separating us from the land. For us, as Native Hawaiians, the land is an ancestor. It's a grandparent. You just don't sell your grandmother."

And you saw it in the summer of 2018, when news spread that the Chicago-based restaurant chain Aloha Poke—founded and run by white men from the continental United States—was sending cease and desist orders to other restaurants that used the words "aloha" and "poke" in their names. "I keep hearing today about this guy in the Midwest, not Hawaiian, who owns a chain of poke shops," said Kaniela Ing, a South Maui legislator and Democrat who unsuccessfully ran for Congress in 2018, in a video he posted on Twitter. "He's suing other shops, or threatening lawsuit, for using the word 'aloha' . . . Now, you know, it's bad enough that that word has been used, commodified, over time, but this is the next level. To think that you have legal ownership over one of the most profound Hawaiian values, it's just something else."

Of course, it isn't just white people who feel the right to take what they wish from Hawaiian culture and history. The box office superstar Dwayne

"The Rock" Johnson (who was born in Hayward, California, and is of Samoan, not Hawaiian, descent) has been lobbying studios for over a decade to play Kamehameha—the Kanaka warrior who finally united the Hawaiian Islands in the late eighteenth century—in a big-budget film.

"The argument that Johnson, as a Samoan, possesses the requisite ancestry to represent Hawaiians and Hawaiian-ness is ethically dubious," the journalist and sovereignty activist Anna Keala Kelly wrote in her 2003 essay "Haolewood: Colonial Codes, Kapu Narratives, and Kanaka 'Ōiwi Discourse" when news of the film project first surfaced. "The assertion that his Polynesian-ness gives the producers the 'right' to do this film is based on American hierarchical ideals that have as much to do with the legacy of America's caste system, as it does with the tradition of casting complicit non-natives in politically contested spaces. In this Sony Pictures film about one of the most important Hawaiian political and historical figures, the neo-colonial code has already been reinforced before one frame of film has moved through the gate."

And, in a way, it's what I was doing as editor of *Maui Time*. I wasn't from Maui or Hawai'i, yet I was in charge of a publication purporting to tell residents what was important on the island. I knew how to craft an article—how to find sources, conduct interviews, do public records research and arrange words into sentences, and then paragraphs—but my knowledge of Hawaiian history was minimal and Hawaiian language nil, beyond simple words like mauka and makai that honestly every tourist should learn before they step off the plane. My first years as editor were quiet, owed partly to the paper's still-low profile as well as whatever journalistic skills I possessed, but at some point, my own ignorance would get me into trouble.

CHAPTER 5

KIANA DAVENPORT

Unlike Oʻahu, Kauaʻi and Hawaiʻi Island, there are no major military installations on Maui. But especially in Lahaina, where *Maui Time* was located in the early 2000s, you could see the military presence in Hawaiʻi up close. U.S. Navy frigates, destroyers and submarines would anchor in Lahaina Roads just offshore of town, and sailors would, as they had for over a century, venture into Lahaina on liberty. They were easy to spot in local bars—arms bulging in polo shirts, giant watches on their wrists. Sometimes Air Force fighter jets would fly low over the channel separating Maui from Lānaʻi. None of it was heavy or particularly intrusive, but it was consistent.

The novelist Kiana Davenport was, and remains, one of the sharpest critics of the military presence in Hawaiʻi. I was a couple years into my job at *MauiTime* when she wrote *House of Many Gods*. When she went on a book tour that included a stop on Maui, I decided to give her, and her spot-on indictment of the militarization of Hawaiʻi, some well-deserved publicity. And this was a couple decades before the U.S. Navy allowed leaking fuel tanks to poison the aquifers supplying drinking water to hundreds of thousands of residents on Oʻahu—a nightmare that will take many years to resolve.

Hawaiʻi's relationship with the U.S. military is complex. Marines played a key role in the overthrow of the Hawaiian Kingdom, and the U.S. government made the island chain a territory at the close of the Spanish–American War to provide a strategic coaling port for the Navy. Today, huge bases take up thousands of acres on Kauaʻi, Oʻahu and Hawaiʻi Island. Gunnery practice obliterated parts of the Koʻolau range on Oʻahu, while barrels full of chemical weapons from World War I sit in the ocean just offshore. Navy pilots practiced so much bombing on the island of Kahoʻolawe that they shattered the island's water table, making future human habitation there extremely difficult.

Despite this, Hawaiʻi has been so thoroughly integrated into the United States since the early twentieth century that generations of people with Hawaiian lineage have served honorably in all branches of the armed forces. Davenport explores this paradox in a scene about a third of the way into *House of Many Gods* where a hundred Native Hawaiian anti-war activists try to protest U.S. military bombings and maneuvers on Oʻahu's Waiʻanae coast. Led by a disabled Vietnam vet named Lopaka, the demonstrators attempt to unfurl huge banners saying "NO MORE MILITARY BOMBING" and "GET OFF OUR SACRED LANDS" while bombs explode in the nearby Mākua Valley. The cops who start cracking their heads are Hawaiian, too.

"You're a brother," the main character, Ana, asks one of the indifferent cops. "How can you do this?"

This Machiavellian pitting of Hawaiian against Hawaiian while American troops practice invasion tactics in the background is a brutal indictment of U.S. rule over Hawaiʻi—which has always been pretty much low-key violent from the 1893 overthrow to the present. That the scene takes place in a lush work of romantic fiction is stunning. Complex and unforgiving, tragic and yet still hopeful, *House of Many Gods* is also one of the sharpest and most articulate arguments yet made against the U.S. military's running roughshod over Hawaiʻi.

It's not completely hyperbolic to say there are a million things going on in Davenport's novel, her third after the critically acclaimed *Shark Dialogues* in 1994 and *Song of the Exile* in 1999. Ostensibly the tale of a fiery Hawaiian woman and her estranged mother, the story has interludes on the conflict between Native Hawaiian culture with Western religions, Russian environmental degradation, San Francisco, illegitimate children, cancer, traditional Hawaiian childbirth techniques, 1950s nuclear testing, crime, Waiʻanae poverty, the Moscow Circus, the horrors of a teaching hospital's emergency room, Vietnam vets who turn against war, anger management and Hurricane ʻIniki.

Any one of those ideas could easily fill *House of Many God's* 330 pages. Most are touched on briefly, but running consistently throughout the story is the struggle against the American military's often heavy-handed presence. Davenport's bitterness at the Pentagon was sometimes as heavy-handed as the Army's exploding bombs.

"These lands are our lands," Lopaka lectures an army guard at one point. "You stole them from us. You're storing nuclear weapons here. You're testing bombs up the highway at Makua. You think we're stupid? We don't know? . . . You think this is what I fought for? To watch my homelands blown to bits?"

A hapa haole from Oʻahu, Davenport insisted that everything in her book is based on fact. In fact, she says her Oʻahu cousins have been demonstrating against the military in Mākua Valley for years.

"Just this week, I was looking at the papers—they want more live fire training," she told me during our 2006 interview. "And more landfills. They're just dumping things out there—where the poorest and least educated Hawaiians live. It just infuriates me. Five percent of the population, but they get 95 percent of the dumpsites. I know we do need to be alert, but Jesus—they're supposed to be protecting the people. What's going on in certain areas is not advantageous to the people."

Actually, it's more than just certain areas. Military weapons training and maneuvers run throughout the Hawaiian Islands. On the Big Island, the U.S. Army wants a huge swath of territory to train crews in using its "Stryker" armored vehicles. The U.S. Navy has a missile test range at Barking Sands, Kauaʻi. The Navy's been gone from Kahoʻolawe for a while now, but its presence—in the form of tons of unexploded ordnance—will remain for many decades to come. In fact, shattered bombs and spent depleted uranium bullets litter much of the Hawaiian Islands.

This is not a new phenomenon. We now know, for example, that in the mid-1940s, the U.S. Army dumped tens of thousands of bombs—totaling perhaps 15 million pounds—containing mustard gas and other chemical weapons into the water barely five miles off the Waiʻanae coast.

Exactly where all the warheads are, and their present state, remains a mystery. Apparently, military records concerning weapons dumpings are pretty much nonexistent, or so the Pentagon claims. In fact, pressure from Oʻahu's U.S. Representative Neil Abercrombie (who later became a one-term Hawaiʻi governor) and U.S. Senator Daniel Akaka, who died in 2018, got the Pentagon to finally start studying the long-term health and environmental effects of the gas warhead dumpings.

At various times in *House of Many Gods,* characters talk of nuclear weapons stored in Mākua Valley. The Red Hill ordnance depot on Oʻahu has also long been a rumored home to the worst weapons in the U.S. arsenal. Because of the understandable paranoia that grips the U.S. government concerning nuclear weapons, the presence of such weapons remains a matter of conjecture.

"It is the policy of the U.S. government to neither confirm nor deny the presence or absence of nuclear weapons at any general or specific location," is how any member of the military is to answer any question regarding the alleged storage of nuclear weapons at any U.S. military base.

The reason is national security—we don't want our enemies to have any advantage in finding our doomsday weapons. The logic is inescapable. But in the rush to "protect" the American people, health and environmental security for those who live near those weapons ends up getting sacrificed.

"Cancer seems to be rampant on the Wainaie [sic] Coast, along with respiratory diseases," Davenport said. Indeed, her novel is filled with gripping instances of people dealing with "da Big C."

For a love story, death is a constant throughout *House of Many Gods*. Characters come and go, but always in the background, army bombs go off. Indeed, drama seems to ebb and flow, depending on whether the army is training for amphibious warfare.

"The book took longer than it should have," Davenport said, adding that the book went through 24 drafts. "What stopped me cold was 9/11—I lost four friends in that. I was in hospitals looking for them for weeks. I didn't write for a year. With all that's happening in the world, you wonder why you write fiction. Do you know what I mean? Why does anybody bother writing fiction anymore? The world seems so unbelievable."

This was a full decade before Donald Trump got elected to the White House. But understanding Americans animated by greed and white supremacy is something Hawaiian people understand far better than the rest of us.

Chapter 6

CALVIN KUAMOʻO

I can't talk about Hawaiians and the U.S. military without talking about Calvin Kuamoʻo, one of the most extraordinary people I ever met on Maui. He died in Wailuku in December 2018 at the age of 70. A little over a year prior, I sat down with him for a story—not the one I originally planned on, but that often happens in journalism. His niece Shan worked for the paper as an administrator, and I had asked her if I could talk to him about his work as a kind of citizen journalist, going around the island to film various sporting and cultural events, which he would then post on his YouTube channel. He was everywhere—high school volleyball matches, basketball games and swim meets. Hawaiian music concerts at the Baldwin Home and Picnic with Poki shows at Kaʻahumanu Church. He also filmed the island's Friday town parties as well as various community events. His Kanaka Cam channel on YouTube boasted more than 100 videos shot over the previous year. Each opened the same, with an extreme close-up of his eyes.

At first, Calvin politely declined, but then, a few days later, Shan told me Calvin was suddenly ready to talk. He came by our office shortly thereafter, which would have been August of 2017. During our chat, Calvin did most of the talking, which was perfectly fine by me. To my surprise, Calvin didn't really want to talk about Maui—he wanted to talk about Vietnam. While he ultimately answered my question about why he films so many events, he could only do so by talking about his experiences as an infantry soldier with the 75th Ranger Regiment during the Vietnam War.

"I remember Calvin well," said Rick Grimes, who served with Kuamoʻo and maintains an online archive of photos of the unit's Vietnam experiences. "He was well-liked, and the other Rangers knew they could depend on him in the most difficult situations. A true American hero, a great asset to the 75th Rangers and I was proud to serve with him."

Calvin said he got interested in filming when he was a young man and saw a neighbor doing an 8mm recording. "I was really excited about that," he told me. "He captured my family. In those days, we couldn't afford cameras. There weren't too many Hawaiians with cameras then."

It was about 1966. Soon after, Calvin said he left for Alaska aboard a United States Geological Survey ship. Though his draft status in high school had been classified 4F, it had raised to 1C when he joined the ship. To him, that meant he could get into the military. The first week of January 1969, he joined the U.S. Army.

"I wanted to get there as soon as possible," Calvin said.

"Get where?" I asked.

"Over to Vietnam," he said. "I knew at some point that the war was going to stop. When I went to Alaska, my cousin also left for Vietnam. Everyone was leaving except for me."

This surprised me. "Were you afraid of being left out?" I asked.

"It was not about being left out," he said flatly. "It was about doing what's right. An undeclared war was a great opportunity for me to learn. I'd been hearing a lot of news about it. I wanted to be there to do a part. I was 21 when I joined. I had just made 21."

After enlisting, Calvin attended Basic Training at Fort Jackson in South Carolina, Advanced Infantry Training at Camp Crockett in Georgia and then Jump School at Fort Benning, Georgia. Around the Fourth of July, he took a plane home to Hawai'i to see his family. After the visit, he let them drive him to the airport. Once there, he went into a restroom and changed into his uniform. When he came out, he thought his mother was going to have a heart attack. "She ran and grabbed a pocket Bible for me," he said. "My mom, she was so funny."

Calvin met another airborne soldier named Timothy on the flight out of Hickam Air Field, and they quickly became friends. But once they got to Vietnam, Calvin said he and Timothy, who had just gotten married a few weeks prior, had to wait for their orders. And wait. And wait.

Bored one night, Calvin said he told Timothy he wanted to cross the street to where the non-airborne soldiers were housed because they had a swimming pool. Timothy thought it was a bad idea because they were specifically ordered to stick to their side of the street. "But we all look alike," Calvin said, so they crossed the street and snuck in to see a movie. It was then that the alert was sounded.

Because the base was now on alert, Calvin said he and Timothy could get shot if they tried to make it back to their side of the compound. But seeing as how the pool looked good, they took off their uniforms and got in until the all-clear was sounded. When it was, they emerged, dressed, and made it back to their position. But their sergeant was waiting for them, Calvin said, and he ordered them to report for "extra duty," which in their case meant burning shit.

"Boy, was I pissed," Calvin said. But then at lunch, a command sergeant major came in, looking for recruits for the 75th Rangers Regiment. He wanted volunteers, he said, because they just lost a team.

"I raised my arm," Calvin said. He told Timothy to raise his arm, too.

"No," he said. "They just lost a team!"

Undeterred, Calvin said he knocked Timothy's hand up, volunteering him as well.

Calvin had volunteered because joining the unit meant no more extra duty like burning shit. But it also meant more danger. His patriotism had gotten him to Vietnam, Calvin said, but once there, he found himself sent way down south to An Khê, where he was a foreigner, an aggressor, in an undeclared war. He was shooting at people who were fighting for their country. Eventually his unit was sent elsewhere, to places like Pleiku and Da Lat, a former French resort. "Da Lat is lovely," Calvin said. "Everybody speaks French. It had gas stations, restaurants, spas and an outdoor pond where you could take out pedal boats. That was the first time I had a shishkebab. I was very impressed."

Though Calvin described being in Da Lat almost like he was a tourist, he also said it was there that he ended up descending into the storm drains after smelling a "distinct" odor. There, he found what he called a "city beneath the city": fortified Viet Cong positions and bunkers. But there was no firefight, he said, because everyone was surprised. "As long as we didn't fire, they wouldn't," he said. "There was a lot of guessing on our part."

Eventually, Calvin said his unit settled on a routine: four days in the field, then three days back at base. While in the field, Calvin said his unit developed almost a game, using a camera belonging to one of the soldiers. "It was a Nikon," Calvin recalled. "Everybody used it. We took turns."

What Calvin described next still haunts me. He said the soldier with the Nikon would wait for the enemy to come down the trail, then he'd jump up, snap a picture, then pull out his weapon and fire. "You snap the picture, then you draw," he said. "High risk. But to be in that mode, and to take a camera, was the greatest feeling. The hunt was over now."

Timothy's tour was up a few months before Calvin's. After the war, Calvin said he was called both a baby-killer, because he'd been in the army, and a draft-dodger, because he had long hair. After returning home to see his family, he ended up in the Southwest, visiting some of his army buddies. Eventually they made their way to Sulfur, Oklahoma, where he was busted for possessing a pound and a half of marijuana, which he said he ate before the cops arrested him. In any case, he said he was sentenced to four months in jail. As he was still in the army, he was then handed over to the military police. Not long after, he was discharged.

"I was a mess," Calvin told me. "Coming home, my parents, grandparents, aunts, uncles, cousins all contributed to my well-being. But it was a struggle. I still have a lot of flash memories when I'm walking about. Sometimes, when I'm driving, I have to grab myself and pull over to the side. I'm still dealing with it. Filming events helps me focus on the here and now, but it's very easy to drift into the past. The mountains look similar, some of the people look similar. But being in the community helps me focus on the here and now."

Chapter 7

HARMING THE SOUL

For my first few years as *Maui Time* editor, the paper was located in Lahaina. The two friends who'd founded the paper about seven years earlier had lived there, so it made sense to set up shop there. By the time I hired in, the paper's office was on the second floor of the 505 Front Street shopping complex, which sat near the southern edge of town and offered ocean-view windows and a view of a nightly $100/person luau. Monday through Friday, I parked my car in the dungeon-like underground parking garage and walked upstairs, made calls and wrote until about one in the afternoon, then walked a few blocks into the town itself for lunch.

Before the August 8 fire, which obliterated virtually everything I just described, Lahaina was promoted by local tourism officials as a "historic whaling town." When I first moved to Maui, the brig *Carthaginian II*, an old German freight-carrying vessel from the late nineteenth century remanufactured to look like a nineteenth-century whaler, was still tied up in Lahaina Harbor, though it was closed and slated to be sunk as an artificial reef just off the coast of Launiupoko, where it would be a new tourist attraction for divers. Other historic spots around town, like the old courthouse, Pioneer Inn, Seafarer's Hospital and Baldwin Home, all functioned as little town museums, paying homage to the town's supposed importance as a preeminent whaling town in the mid-nineteenth century.

In fact, much of it was bunk. "Lahaina was built and preserved to mimic a whaling town so that tourists vacationing at the newly built Kāʻanapali Beach Resort could visit after long days of rest and relaxation," Sydney Iaukea wrote in 2016. "However, the whaling tale that was recreated had very little in common with the actual industry that existed a century and a half prior. As this whaling historical record was foregrounded, all other social narratives of Lahaina took a back seat, with the missionary influence vying for a close second." Lahaina, as Iaukea noted, was only really a whaling town between the years 1842 and 1860. What's more, none of the buildings on Front Street were specific to the whaling industry (in fact, just one actual whaling structure remains in the entire town—the Spring House, located near the Wharf Cinema Center). That's why, as Iaukea wryly noted, the architectural design guidelines for the Lahaina Historic District mandate "Nantucket" and "Victorian" styles.

Lahaina was a plantation town, built literally on the bones of the old Hawaiian Kingdom's capital—Mokuʻula, which featured a small island constructed in the middle of freshwater ponds, fed by streams running down from the West Maui Mountains. Of course, Pioneer Mill got rid of all that. "This rich natural environment existed for centuries before the Pioneer Mill Company installed vast irrigation systems in West Maui that diverted most of the fresh water across the plains to the drier areas for sugar cane production," Iaukea wrote. "These massive water diversion projects produced stagnant waters, which are said to have introduced mosquitoes in Lahaina." After using Mokuʻula for "dumping grounds," Iaukea wrote, Pioneer Mill covered it with a baseball field, which remains there to this day. A renewed emphasis on Lahaina's pre-contact history, as well as increased study of Mokuʻula itself, was beginning when I left Maui for the last time. While good, the desire to draw tourist attention—and dollars—to this history was unquestionably part of the calculation.

The need for more tourists, and specifically more tourists who spend money, is insatiable not just on Maui, but throughout Hawaiʻi. But selling Hawaiʻi as an attraction to outsiders harms the soul of Hawaiians, as the late Rev. Abraham Akaka predicted in his famous 1959 sermon, delivered when Hawaiʻi became the 50th state:

> There are fears that Hawaiʻi as a state will be motivated by economic greed; that statehood will turn Hawaiʻi (as someone has said) into a great big spiritual junkyard filled with smashed dreams, worn-out illusions; that it will make the Hawaiian people lonely, confused, insecure, empty, anxious, restless, disillusioned—a wistful people.

Activists Haunani Kay Trask and Mililani Trask used the word "prostitution" to describe the effect tourism would have on Hawaiʻi, and they damn well meant it:

Hawaiian women dance with Hawaiian men at "lu'aus" for a lavish "island" buffet and "thrilling" Polynesian revue. Needless to say, Hawaiians don't participate, and didn't participate in such things before the advent of haoles in the islands. The woman has an innocent look and is portrayed as a costumed maiden who is virginal yet enticing to the haole tourists. In the native tradition, the hula was performed: 1) as a Mohai (sacred offering); 2) to transmit knowledge as a component of the oral traditions; and 3) as a vehicle for providing social and cultural cohesion. Tourism ponders sexuality through the hula—it commodifies the hula for the lurid gratification of the haole.

This can, and has, led to actual violence. It's an issue I still regret not pursuing while I was *MauiTime* editor. Eventually the paper's office moved to Wailuku, and I moved to Kīhei, in South Maui. Often, I would pass by a World War II–era bunker in Central Maui that was frequently graffitied with the names of missing local women. I never took the time to research these painful, entirely avoidable tragedies. Missing indigenous women are more than a plot point on television programs like *Alaska Daily*—in Hawai'i, such cases are all too plentiful, and I could easily have covered such cases for *MauiTime*, though it was only after I left the island that I realized just how necessary journalism was to generate awareness of the crimes. Thankfully, others, like the state's Office of Hawaiian Affairs (OHA) and Commission on the Status of Women, have done a great deal to promote missing Hawaiian women in recent years.

In December 2022, Hawai'i's Missing and Murdered Native Hawaiian Women and Girls task force released a 23-page report on the matter. Titled "HOLOI Ā NALO WĀHINE 'ŌIWI" (roughly translates as "delete and lose Hawaiian women") and edited by individuals from both OHA and the Status of Women commission, the report detailed tragic cases of trafficking and murder that stretch across all the Hawaiian Islands. "Indigenous women and girls, including Native Hawaiians, experience violence at much higher rates than other populations in the United States," states the report. "A shocking 84.3% of Indigenous women experience violence in their lifetime." Indeed, Indigenous women and girls are 10 times more likely to get murdered than women of other ethnic groups, according to the report.

The reason for such disproportionate violence was simple: colonization, which brought Western patriarchal power structures, prostitution and sexually transmitted diseases for which Kānaka Maoli had no immunity, according to the report. The report also makes clear that colonization continues to grip Hawai'i through "the heavy military presence and land holdings in Hawai'i and capitalism via the domination of the tourism industry." This harms Kānaka Maoli in a variety of realms, including economics, education, mental and physical health, and crime, according to the report. Of the latter, the reason behind the report, the worst damage is done, on average, to teen girls. In fact, of the 37 cases of missing children reported between 2020 and 2022 by the Missing Children's Center Hawai'i, the average age of the missing child is 15, 77 percent are female, 84 percent are Native Hawaiian, and 71 percent disappeared on O'ahu, the island on which most people in Hawai'i live, according to the report.

Statistics like this are genuinely appalling, and though they were long ignored (or at least not examined), that's no longer the case. In 2022, U.S. Senator Mazie Hirono (D-Hawai'i) introduced a bill to amend the Violence Against Women Act to better ensure that Native Hawaiian organizations are able to assist the community. In late December of that year, President Joe Biden signed the bill into law. "Like other Native communities across the country, Native Hawaiians experience disproportionately high levels of sexual and gender-based violence," said Senator Hirono in a December 28, 2022, news release. "Despite this crisis, Native Hawaiian women have long been unjustly excluded from accessing much-needed resources for survivors provided through the Violence Against Women Act. This bill addresses this injustice and allows Native Hawaiian organizations to better serve Native Hawaiians, and I'm glad the President has signed it into law. Now, Native Hawaiian organizations will have access to support and resources to serve the Native Hawaiian community and work towards eradicating sexual violence in our state."

* * *

Still, the demands of tourism remain, and they are insatiable: quantity inevitably surrenders to quality, as more visitors endlessly demand access to better, more "authentic" experiences. Around 2014, I started hearing a lot of officials—local, state and federal—talking about "cultural heritage tourism." This was tourism geared to the "real" Hawai'i—no more manufactured, cartoonish experiences. Visitors wanted to live Hawai'i as real Hawaiians did, though who exactly defined "real Hawaiians" was up for grabs. But it had to happen, these officials said, because the dollar signs were too big to ignore. "Most studies, even those that go back 20 or more years, show that cultural and heritage tourists spend 150 percent more than other tourists," tourism expert Andrew Witt told *Pacific Business News* that year.

Put simply, luaus filled with Tahitian dancing and prime rib were out, experiences based on local Hawai'i food and traditions were in. U.S. Senator

Brian Schatz may have meant well in 2018 when he introduced a bill expanding cultural heritage tourism throughout Hawai'i, but the damage done to local history and culture by such tourism is incalculable. "This bill is about returning control to the people who live in the places everyone else wants to visit," stated a news release put out by Schatz's office on the bill. "It gives local communities the chance to see more benefits from tourism, including better jobs, and it puts the story of Hawai'i in the hands of our own residents. This is what international visitors and tourists are looking for—authentic experiences that tell a story and have a history."

But commodification is still commodification—changing who gets the money after the transaction doesn't alter the transaction itself. And even with such assurances, it still doesn't mean the tourism establishment will accept a new hierarchy.

Case in point is the Council for Native Hawaiian Advancement (CNHA), a nonprofit based on O'ahu that's dedicated to advancing the economic and political development of Native Hawaiians. In late 2022, the CNHA protested the Hawai'i Tourism Authority (HTA), a state agency, when it granted a lucrative tourism marketing contract to the Hawai'i Visitors and Convention Bureau, which has long dominated the tourism marketing industry in Hawai'i. To everyone's surprise, the HTA rescinded the contract and put the whole thing out to bid, which the CNHA won. But then the Convention and Visitors Bureau cried foul, putting the whole thing on hold. During state Senate hearings on the matter, a state official named Mike McCartney took the blame for the whole snafu. At the time, McCartney was head of the state agency that oversees the HTA, but in the past he had worked as HTA chairman as well as chief of staff to then-Governor David Ige, exemplifying the deep connections between the tourism industry and state and local government. And this was just a fight over who gets a tourism marketing contract, showing the nearly insurmountable cliff that stands before anyone attempting to question the need for tourism marketing in the first place.

Chapter 8

PRISON

As of 2010, according to the state Office of Hawaiian Affairs (OHA), there were "an overwhelming number" of Native Hawaiian men and women incarcerated in prison, in both the State of Hawai'i and the continental United States. "It is clear that when a Native Hawaiian person enters the criminal justice system, they serve more time in prison and more time on probation than other racial or ethnic groups," according to an OHA report on incarceration released that year. "Native Hawaiians are also likely to have their parole revoked and be returned to prison compared to other racial or ethnic groups." The indigenous people of Hawai'i, OHA noted, were caught in a cycle of imprisonment that spanned generations. Though OHA's findings are now over a decade old, they remain valid. In fact, researcher John Taschner found in 2021 that the "historically" high rate of incarceration was disproportionately costing Native Hawaiian prison inmates their lives during the first year of the COVID-19 pandemic.

Reporting on local people in Hawai'i was, to a great extent, writing about incarceration. To my amazement, at least in the early 2000s, there were state and local officials trying to reform the incarceration cycle that too often chewed up generations of local residents.

One such example was Betsy Duncombe's yoga class at Maui Community Correctional Center (MCCC), which I visited in February of 2004 and which usually included 18 to 22 guys. They filed in every Tuesday and Thursday, always at least a couple minutes before the 8:30 a.m. start time. They came wearing t-shirts and shorts or even jeans. Most were in slippers, though some chose to come to class in work boots. Some stretched on worn mats, but most simply spread out on white towels.

When I first saw them, they were all lying on their stomachs, trying to arch their backs as far as they could. "For those of you in this posture," said Duncombe, "feel how wide open your lungs are."

The guys grunted and strained and coughed. Most couldn't bend their backs more than a few inches, but some managed to get their heads pointed almost straight up, their eyes closed in sublime relaxation.

Duncombe then asked the guys to turn over onto their backs—a request they happily carried out. Lying flat on her back, she then raised both her upper body and her legs off the ground, bending her body into a V. The older guys closest to her looked aghast. Just one guy succeeded in duplicating her effort.

A few moments later, they were kneeling, bending their arms above their heads.

"The center of this practice is non-aggression," says Duncombe.

"I smell perfume," one guy near the back said, shattering the room's silence.

Duncombe ignored him. "There's a way to achieve strength without doing harm," she said. "To push ourselves to the edge without pushing beyond it."

Known as Free Inside, Duncombe's experimental yoga class for inmates was unique at that time, though others (including one of my former freelance writers) later replicated her efforts. Duncombe's students were, for the most part, nearing the end of their sentences—in some cases 10 to 15 years. Their convictions were harsh and included murder, assault, rape and drug trafficking.

About four months old, the course was part of a research study Duncombe was conducting as part of her University of Hawai'i master's degree work. Having already taught one 12-week class the previous year, Duncombe was now in the third week of her next group of students. As far as anyone close to the program could tell, Free Inside was one of the only attempts anywhere in the United States at using ancient yoga, chi gung and meditative techniques to rehabilitate prisoners. Its goals, as written out in Duncombe's guidebook, were ambitious: "Lower recidivism in its inmate participants; lower staff turnover . . . improve the physical and mental health of all its participants; result in calmer, kinder prison behavior in all of its participants; improve reunification success of paroled inmate participants with their families and employers."

"When you see the interconnectedness of people, it's very hard to go out and hurt people," said Duncombe. "I'm just getting them to a place within themselves that they may have lost touch with. But no matter what I see in these guys, it's what they do under stress that counts. What's important is making habitual what they learn in this class."

Duncombe told me that something like 70 percent of released prisoners continue to commit crimes, eventually ending up back behind bars. For many decades, centuries even, Western correctional thinking has focused on the punishment aspects of incarceration—beating down and isolating prisoners. With so few "reformed criminals" coming out of prison these days, it would seem something isn't working.

I sat down with Duncombe a week before visiting her MCCC class. She was a slight 43-year-old woman with brown hair and green eyes. Married to a local radio disc jockey, she had two daughters, aged eight and 17.

"I'm aware of my white imperialist roots," she said, curled up in a chair beneath a ladder leading to the loft of her Haiku home. "We've done a lot of damage around the world. But I grew up in a family of human rights activists. On the plane to Maui I made a promise—I kid you not—that I would give back."

Duncombe, who at that point had been practicing yoga for two decades, also taught a yoga class at the homeless shelter next to the prison. Like the MCCC inmates, many of her students have a history of drug abuse. But that wasn't new to her. "When I was in my early 20s, I used drugs more than was healthy," she said. She credits her discovery of yoga and meditation with pulling her "out of a very dark place." During her class, Duncombe referenced that past.

"It's important for me to relate to the inmates," she said. "Otherwise, they might assume I read all this in a book."

Yoga is thousands of years old. It is really quite simple, actually—just a series of meditative exercises designed to heal the body physically and mentally. "Meditation helps people to do nothing," said Evaon Wong-Kim, an assistant professor of social work at San Jose State University who was advising Duncombe on her Free Inside project. "It clears their mind. You come to a place where you can see what you've been doing."

Both Duncombe and Wong-Kim pointed out that prison ought to be the ideal place for yoga—lots of people with emotional and physical problems who have a lot of time to practice. Duncombe interviewed her students when the course began, asking them questions they've likely never faced before:

What do you think of this world?
What kind of changes can you make?
Do you feel connected to other people?

At the course's conclusion, Duncombe would ask the same questions again and then compare the results, which she'd then write up in hopes of attracting state or federal funding.

I asked Wong-Kim how they could test effectiveness.

"Consider this the starting point of a larger program," she said. "Just a pilot project."

MCCC Deputy Warden Alan Nouchi joined me when I visited the prison. "Busy day today!" he said a half hour before Duncombe's class began. Short with a mop of dark hair reminiscent of the early Beatles, Nouchi agreed to escort Duncombe, a photographer and myself over to Dorm 6/7 for the morning's class. Though "deputy" remained in his title, Nouchi had been overall head of the prison since the previous June, when then-warden Albert Murashige got himself arrested on four charges of sexually assaulting a female inmate. He later pleaded no contest. Nouchi had been on the MCCC staff for the previous 28 years. Things have changed a lot since he began, he said.

"Today's headcount is 366," he said, looking at the daily roster at the front desk of the gatehouse. "We're rated to hold 209. Even that's a lot more than when I started, which was 16."

"Sixty?!" said the desk guard. "Wow."

"No, 16," Nouchi said. "One-six."

The guard's eyes bugged out.

For a prison official with so many years' experience in corrections, Nouchi—as well as MCCC Programming Director James Hirano, who did a lot to guide Duncombe into the prison—was remarkably open-minded about Duncombe's course. "I'm willing to try anything that could possibly reduce recidivism rates," he said. "If it can change peoples' lives, so be it, man. More power to her. Whatever works. I'm willing to try anything."

After exchanging our driver's licenses for yellow visitor badges, the desk guard electronically unlocked the gatehouse's back door, leading us into a small cage. After the gatehouse door closed, he unlocked the cage door, allowing us access onto the prison yard. Walking down a short road to another locked gate, we crossed a basketball court that offered a tremendous view of Wailuku Heights to get to a plus-sign-shaped building known as Dorm 6/7. Inside are individual showers, bookshelves and other recreational facilities. In the center is another desk, always staffed by two guards. From there, the guards can see directly into the dining room, which is where Duncombe taught her class.

Within a few minutes of her arrival, two incarcerated individuals stacked the dining room's brown metal folding chairs against the wall and began mopping the floor. Duncombe placed a sign-in sheet near the door as her students began filing in. Assigned to the class at random, they would otherwise be on prison work detail at this hour. One student, Jason Camara, brought a couple colorful drawings for an artistic and literary journal Duncombe also publishes. One sheet showed an elaborate pink turtle, while the other displayed an intricately drawn bamboo forest outlining a large heart with the caption "A heart of bamboo/It splits and shatters/But doesn't break!!"

"It clears my mind," Camara said when I asked him about his involvement in the class. "Because of the class, I've started to get into Chinese calligraphy. And a lot of spiritual things."

"All the time I forget these are criminals," Duncombe had told me earlier. "Then the guys will talk about having bullets in them. I see a lot of tears and remorse in their eyes. And a lot of wisdom. I hope they start a daily practice that they don't forget when they're back on the street and tempted in different ways."

I asked her how receptive they were to her presence and teachings.

"They put up a lot of resistance at first," she said. "There are a lot of tough guys, but also a lot of jokesters. I don't take them very seriously. To be honest, I haven't been concerned about my safety."

Duncombe said she'd only cried once during a class. It was December, when she told the students she wanted to teach a class on Christmas. "A few of my usual jokesters said something like it was the last thing they wanted," she said. "I turned around and tried to pull myself together. But then they got concerned. They saw me as a human being instead of a teacher."

"When you drink the water, remember its source," Duncombe said a number of times during her class. The students listened, but said nothing. The room was quiet during the class but periodically interrupted by birds chirping outside or a guard's squawking radio. Every few minutes, a guard walked through the room, carefully stepping over the mats. Duncombe spoke to her students constantly, explaining which organs the various poses helped or the importance of meditation.

"Gather strength from your breath like it's food."

"Sit in a way to feel balanced."

"The tongue corresponds to the heart, sends energy to the heart."

At one point, while discussing the lungs, she asked her students what object in nature the organs resemble. Like a high school class, the students began shouting out all sorts of answers: "Sponge . . . fungus . . . mushrooms . . . cauliflower . . . asparagus . . . artichokes. . . ."

"You know if you spread out the lungs they'll cover a whole tennis court," one guy who hadn't spoken before said, pretty much ending the discussion.

Then they began meditation, which would be tough for any yoga student, considering the patrolling guards and kitchen sounds and occasionally blaring radio.

"We've been using physical means to access our organs," Duncombe said. "In meditation we're using our minds. This is something that is accessible to everyone. The reason this isn't taught in school today, in my opinion, is that there isn't a way to make a profit."

Most students sat cross-legged, but only a few closed their eyes and seemed to slow their thinking. Duncombe then asked her students to think of a time when they were at peace.

"Every time you breathe out, breathe that feeling out," she said. "Breathe in physical pain, then exhale that feeling of peace. We are inviting pain right into our body . . . but we have the ability to transform it."

She asked them to breathe in the pain of someone they love. Then someone they didn't like. Then someone they didn't know. "The ultimate way to heal ourselves," she told them, "is to help other people."

Class ended a few minutes later. The students hurriedly put their mats and towels in a closet, then departed. Duncombe thanked her students and the guards, picked up her clipboard and left, walking back the way she came. Exiting was simply a matter of passing through two more locked gates. The last one, at the cage leading to the gatehouse, had a small sign posted near the latch that I hadn't noticed as we walked in: "Please do not slam gate. Be gentle."

* * *

Later that year, I met Cheryle and Tania. I had heard about their mile-long walk, which they made every Monday, Tuesday, Wednesday and Friday, and wanted to know more. They walked twice, actually—first at 3:30 p.m. and then again at 6:00 p.m. They walked alone, forbidden from stopping or talking to anyone on the way. Bad things happened to them if it took them more than 30 minutes to get to their destination.

The rules and restrictions that faced Cheryle and Tania were due more to where they walked from than where they were headed. That's because Cheryle and Tania were also incarcerated. Both women, who asked that I only use their first names, were single mothers. Cheryle has four children while Tania has three. They were both in their early 30s and in the middle of five-year prison terms for ice use when I interviewed them.

They were also part of a state Drug Court program called Track Five that allowed them to walk or ride a bike out of prison four days a week to get counseling and treatment at the Cameron Center. Once there, the women and about a half dozen other inmates talked about social behavior, critical thinking, thoughts, feelings, urges, co-dependency and self-esteem.

"I've pretty much accepted that I'm [in prison]," said Cheryle. "The first couple days [in Track Five] I felt crappy. Why are we here? But now I'm okay with that. Sometimes it's crazy—we get here, and we want to go back."

"At first, we were scared to even leave," said Tania. "We've been inside a while."

Both Cheryle and Tania said they've seen family members drive by and stop while they're headed to the Cameron Center. In those cases, the women had to ignore them.

"You have to do the right thing, even when nobody's looking," said Tania.

Cheryle agreed. "It can get overwhelming," she said.

Then-MCCC Acting Warden Alan Nouchi told me there are a couple reasons behind allowing inmates to walk in and out of prison. "It's not feasible for us to run a shuttle service," he said. "If they can walk or pedal their way, it will give us an idea as to the trust factor. We set the time to go and come back. Their custody level enables them to go on their own." They are monitored on their journey, Nouchi said, though not one-to-one. But he did say that one Track Five inmate attempted to ride off the route to meet his girlfriend for "hanky panky." A roving guard caught him almost immediately. His attempt landed him back in lockdown.

Track Five had been in existence just a little over three months when I interviewed Cheryle and Tania. There's currently room at MCCC for 24 males and a dozen females to participate in the program, and they live in Dorms III and V, respectively. It is unprecedented in the State of Hawaiʻi. "It's part of our holistic approach," said Drug Court Administrator Barbara-Ann Keller. "We're rebuilding their lives."

Cheryle and Tania were in the program for 60 days, but were uncertain when they'd finish and be able to transfer into work furlough. Both professed gratitude for getting the chance to clean up their lives. "If they just let us out on parole, I would end up using again," said Tania. "At last we can look at the consequences we face. We are able to function when clean."

I interviewed Cheryle and Tania at the Cameron Center in Kahului, which is close to the jail. Sitting in a classroom with pale green walls and tables arranged in a square, they wore not orange scrubs, but the privileged jeans and t-shirts that came with good behavior. Each woman had been through Drug Court before, but had failed—"relapsed" was how they put it. That's the trade-off for agreeing to Drug Court in the first place: successfully complete many months of rigorous counseling and treatment or go to jail.

Before she got into trouble, Cheryle was a nursing student. Now's she's a convicted felon with two years in MCCC under her belt. In 1999, she was arrested for stealing "clothes, lots and lots of clothes from Sears." She got five years' probation. But while on probation, she said, she came up with a "dirty UA"—a urine analysis that showed the presence of crystal methamphetamine. "I started using at a late age," she said, "at 28, when my relationship of 10 years fell apart. I never did anything before. As soon as I took my first hit, the pain was no longer there. I wanted to smoke, I wanted to do it. I lost all sense of self, responsibility."

They were going to revoke her probation and send her to jail, but first she opted to join Impact, the forerunner of Maui Drug Court. "The first time I got into recovery, my kids were taken away and I thought I had to stop," said Cheryle. "I was clean for a year. Everything was good, everything was fine. As soon as I got them back I relapsed. I got into a relationship with another Drug Court client. I broke a rule. But I also ended up using. It was an unhealthy relationship. I didn't want to be alone. I believed at the time that I loved him, even if it meant going to jail. Now that I think about it, it's crazy. I don't want to make excuses. Having my kids back was overwhelming, having to raise them on your own." Cheryle said she knew she was going to jail, so she kept smoking ice right up to her day in court. Now that she was in prison and getting treatment for her drug addiction, she said, she wanted to get back to nursing after her release.

By comparison, Tania was in MCCC for 13 months. But her story was very similar—arrested for possession of ice in 1999, she was also a former Drug Court dropout. "I was offered to do treatment instead of jail," she said. This was in 2001. "I was hanging out with people I was not supposed to hang out with. Was using and selling drugs. Then I got sanctioned by Drug Court. Somebody told on me. I was sent to MCCC. Had the opportunity to go to Pasadena, to Impact, for residential treatment. I stayed there 90 days. Then I came home, got into trouble again, hanging with people who were using and selling. Then I decided not to go to my court hearing. I was scared. I wasn't ready to go back to jail." She was "on the run" for a few weeks before tiring of "looking over my shoulder. So I packed my bags and went to jail." Before she got into trouble, she was self-employed, cleaning people's homes. She said she would like to go back to that.

Cheryle and Tania were tantalizingly close to freedom, but they were still inmates. Though listening to the women talk, you'd almost think prison wasn't so bad. Sure, when you first go in, you're stuck on an empty floor, 24–7.

All you see are four walls, your bunk, toilet and sink. But their good behavior has bought them access to Dorm V, where they enjoy privileges like not having to wear bright orange scrubs. They can also stay up until 2:30 in the morning on Fridays and Saturdays watching TV. Both were also enrolled in pre-employment courses, as well as being Hula Halau participants. In fact, they danced at the Queen Kaʻahumunu shopping center in Kahului. Of course, the same "can't talk with the other people" restrictions applied, but they did get to dance the hula in public.

That being said, prison also meant that they had very little contact with their children. And they had a lot of children. Cheryle has four children—two boys at the time aged 13 and 11, and two girls, aged nine and five. Of them, Cheryle said the boys were living in Las Vegas with their father. Tania had two daughters, 15 and 14 at the time, who lived in Lahaina with her mother and one 13-year-old son living in Arizona.

But a week after I interviewed them, Cheryle and Tania got to spend two hours eating and playing with at least some of their children as part of a Mother's Day event sponsored by the local nonprofit organization Maui Economic Opportunity and Head Start. They arrived at the MEO offices near the Cameron Center at 3:30 in a big yellow school bus, the only Track Five participants in the group of 24 mothers. In fact, Cheryle and Tania were the first ones off the bus and in Classroom Two. Cheryle found her daughters immediately, but Tania hunted around a bit before finding her child that was able to attend.

As this happened, six guards in civilian clothes deployed to the room's four corners. Warden Nouchi, who came in a few minutes earlier, explained that the guards all volunteered for this duty. "But I will pay them anyway," he told me. "I have to."

The women and children scattered around the room, decorated for Cinco de Mayo but filled with Hawaiian guitar music from two guys playing up front. Many children played, off to the side, at games on the floor. Two boys played a game of oversized checkers while their mother sat cross-legged next to them, watching intently. While some kids and mothers went to the craft tables, Tania and her daughter sat at a table near the center of the room, talking. I walked over and said hello, and Tania introduced me to her daughter. A few minutes later, one of the Head Start volunteers read a prayer. Tania and her daughter stood and listened. Tania put her left arm around her daughter's shoulder, which wasn't easy considering her daughter is a few inches taller than her.

At 4:00 p.m., nine of the inmates lined up near the two guitar players and danced the hula. Cheryle, one of the more experienced mothers, was up front, while rookie Tania danced in the back row. A large card colored with crayons sat directly in front of each of them. "A lullaby was selected," Cheryle told the crowd of inmates, children, guards, MEO staffers and reporters. "It reminds us of when they were babies. Each child is like a rainbow." When the women were finished, they walked out and handed the cards, usually decorated around the theme "I love you," to their children.

Not long after, and standing off to the side, MEO Special Projects Director Tom Blackburn-Rodriguez pointed to one mother in a gray long-sleeved shirt and jeans. "She used to work for us," he said. "Now she's got a job at an auto detailing shop. After a month she got a raise. She's out in 30 days."

We talked briefly about the novelty of having such a visitation event. "Have you seen the line at MCCC on the weekends?" he asked. "People standing out in the sun for hours, waiting. It wears you down. Pretty soon their visits are less regular."

Across the room, Drug Court Administrator Keller was watching one mother and daughter. "Look at that poor girl," she said, referring to one crying girl being comforted by her mother. "She's been crying the whole time."

It was a little after five, shortly after the children busted open a couple piñatas, that the event came to a close. As the guitarists played "Somewhere Over the Rainbow," the inmates began collecting their souvenir photos and roses and cards in preparation for getting back on the bus to MCCC. One woman cradled her baby—there were about half a dozen there that day—for a few moments, then handed the child to a staffer before taking her things and leaving. In the confusion, one staffer handed Keller a crying infant.

Tania, in the center of the room, spent her last few moments talking with her daughter. Cheryle then came over, and they both got their things. Neither was crying as they left the room. But as they got on the bus, Cheryle rushed back inside to retrieve a sweatshirt she'd accidentally left behind. In an act of stunning symmetry that could only have been an accident, the song ended exactly as the last mother left the room and returned to prison.

Chapter 9

SUGAR, PART I

The morning of August 9, when we first got aerial images of the devastation of Lahaina, was surreal and shocking. Looking at a town I used to work in and seeing so few reference points was profoundly disturbing. Not until aerial photos were released, and I was able to zoom in and take my time examining what was left block by block, was I able to appreciate the scale of the disaster. One of the few landmarks left in town was the 200-foot Pioneer Mill smokestack. Located near the intersection of Honoapiʻilani Highway and Lahainaluna Road, the stack now towered over a neighborhood of ashes. The old sugar mill had been torn down years ago, but the stack, which dated to 1928, had been left to remind everyone of the factory that once stood there.

When I first moved to Maui, the mill had been closed for four years, but all the sheds, buildings and offices still remained. Covered in overgrown weeds and broken windows, the corrugated metal buildings looked like some post-nuclear industrial outpost. Thick, rusty pipes seemed to snake along the walls and ceilings for miles. Inside, giant rats scurried along rock mounds and massive steel girders. The sugar fields themselves were bone dry, with only a few active fields of genetically modified seed corn remaining. Before the fire, the site was a light, almost gentle tourist attraction maintained by the Lahaina Restoration Foundation that neglected to mention how the mill itself played an important, even vital, role in white people's colonization of Hawaiʻi. The mill exploited tens of thousands of Hawaiian and immigrant workers and rerouted the centuries-old streams that fed generations of Hawaiʻi farmers, turning the once lush hillsides above and south of Lahaina Town brown.

Sugar production spanned 150 or so years of Hawaiʻi history, but its greatest years stretched from 1840 (when the Hawaiian Kingdom reigned supreme) to 1940 (when the Territory of Hawai'i was converting into a massive military bastion for the United States). In that century, sugar plantations had transformed the islands in ways so deep that they'll be with us forever. "By 1920, sugar had remolded the islands into a production machine that drew extensively on island soils, forests, waters, and its island residents, to satisfy North America's sugar craving," anthropologist Carol MacLennan wrote in her 2014 book *Sovereign Sugar*. "Native communities—human, plant, and animal—adapted, disappeared or found niches in which to survive on a small scale. Imported and transplanted peoples, plants, and animals largely replaced them."

The plantations were sprawling—covering a quarter-million acres by 1920—and required thousands of workers. Because diseases introduced by contact with Europeans in the late 1700s had devastated Native Hawaiians (their numbers dropping from between 279,000 to 800,000 in 1780 to a mere 30,000 by 1900), the plantations imported huge numbers of Japanese, Chinese, Filipino, Puerto Rican and Portuguese workers, forming the "mixed plate" ethnic makeup that makes up Hawai'i today.

Such massive change occurred throughout the state's ecology. Thirsty sugar depleted the soil of nutrients and demanded huge quantities of water through rainfall and irrigation, according to MacLennan. The plantations also harvested whole forests for planting and fuel (though they quickly learned that preservation also served a vital role). In an attempt to control rats, plantation owners imported the mongoose in the 1880s. But that proved to be "environmentally unsound," according to MacLennan, and led to the slaughter of Hawai'i's ground-nesting birds.

By the late 1880s, the plantation owners—who were intertwined with the missionaries who'd gained power after the destruction of the old kapu system in the early 1800s—had themselves grown so powerful that they forced the notorious Bayonet Constitution on King Kalākaua. Its mandate that only property owners could vote meant that two-thirds of Native Hawaiians no longer had a voice over the governing of their own islands.

While Hawai'i has since become a democracy, the power wielded by the sugar barons themselves remained considerable, though they now traffic in land. And what to do with Pioneer Mill's detritus had become a controversial issue in the early 2000s, with locals arguing with locals about what the mill really meant to Lahaina, Maui and Hawai'i.

At the time, most Lahaina residents wanted to save the smokestack. Its structure was one of those things, like the old brig *Carthaginian II* and the Lahainaluna High School "L" on the hill that made the town picturesque.

For much of the twentieth century, it didn't just dump tons of ash and soot on Lahaina, but also served as a landmark for local fishermen venturing out at night. But in 2004, the Kāʻanapali Development Corporation (KDC)—the company that took over the mill from American Factors and had decided that land development north of Lahaina was more profitable than sugar—announced that it would knock the whole complex down except for the stack. This wasn't surprising, considering that the Environmental Protection Agency had labeled the mill a Superfund Site with "higher than normal" levels of toxic lead and arsenic in two areas. KDC said that had all been cleaned up, but still wanted the mill gone, company officials told residents during a June 1, 2004, town hall meeting in a local school auditorium.

"[The company did] many, many, many tests," KDC Vice President A. James Wriston, III told the crowd of about two dozen on June 1. "We found a couple spots. They have all been cleaned up . . . asbestos pulled out . . . lead paint taken out . . . oils, spills—all that has been taken out."

Wriston also admitted that saving the stack depended on a $280,000 refurbishment project and a caretaker agency stepping forward to maintain it. "We've made no promises or commitments on the stack," Wriston told the residents, though he did make clear that the stack would remain for the foreseeable future.

Two men who spoke during that meeting encapsulated the emotional, sometimes bitter divisions that plagued the issue of what to do with the shuttered Pioneer Mill. For one, Wriston's announcement was too little—save all of the old mill, he said, and build a museum to teach future generations about the "economic miracle" the sugar plantation had brought to Maui. For the other, keeping the stack was a dreadful salute to the segregationist, land-stealing commercial interests that replaced the Hawaiian monarchy and society with American imperialist rule. What struck me was how both men framed their arguments in terms of what was best for the Hawaiian people.

Wearing white hair drawn into a ponytail, a long white beard and a bright red Hawai'i Marines t-shirt, Fuzzy Alboro, Sr. (then 74) had spoken at many previous gatherings on the important role the mill had played in Lahaina and Maui history. He also liked to talk about fishing. "When I was young, 20s and 30s, we went fishing," Alboro said at the town hall meeting. "We used the stack as a marker." For many locals, this was the smokestack at its most functional. After all, guys like Alboro were out on the water, fishing in a small boat with no motor or electronic gear. Catching fish was simply a matter of dropping the net, dropping bait into the net and then pulling the net up.

But Alboro said he also had a personal connection to the mill. "If not for the Pioneer Mill, I would never have been able to educate my five children," he said.

Alboro was an unabashed fan of saving as much of the mill as possible. It was an interesting point of view, to say the least, because a few days after that meeting, he told me that the mill had nearly killed him.

"In 1983, I fell in a well that was 100 feet deep," Alboro told me. "I was supposed to be dead. That was the end of my career in sugar." Alboro, working as an electrician, had been inspecting a well near the sewage plant in Honokowai when he fell. He broke a few ribs, punctured his lungs and diaphragm, pushed up his left foot an inch and a half and fractured both legs. Doctors later replaced his hip as well. "I'm happy that I'm still alive," he told me. "I was in Memorial Hospital [in Wailuku] for three months. Then I did rehab in Honolulu for five months, where I learned to walk again."

The injuries had capped a career that dated back to June 20, 1950, when Alboro was first hired as a ditch digger making 89 cents an hour. Except for a couple tours he spent with the 1st Marine Air Wing during the Korean War, Alboro would stay at the mill for 33 years doing, as he put it, "all different kinds of work." Along the way, Alboro did stints as union secretary, shop steward and unit chairman. After digging ditches, Alboro worked planting cane. Then he worked as a fertilizer sprayer. "That was one of the hardest jobs I've ever done," he said. "The more acres you do, the more you get paid. But you have to spray the fertilizer by hand." Later he laid pipes to irrigate the fields. Soon after he took an opening as a pump tender, and he did that about a year. After that he went to the research department, where he did things like determine if there was enough fertilizer in a given field. After that he worked making sure the cane juice was well measured. Then he became an electrician.

While there's no question Alboro worked damn hard at some thankless jobs for three decades, it's also undeniable that the plantation compensated him well. For instance, he told the town hall meeting attendees that he was able to buy a nice home in the company's residential neighborhood for a mere $3,700. For him, the smokestack was a deeply important symbol of everything that went right in his life, even if the mill had not always been kind to him.

"It's just like the Statue of Liberty," Alboro said. "Something goes wrong, you want to take that down? I don't think so!" Then at the meeting, Alboro mentioned a conversation he'd had years prior with his manager about how the mill ought to become a museum.

"That would have been nice," Wriston from the KDC said, his tone indicating that he genuinely thought the idea was nice, but had absolutely no intention of ever acting on it.

As Alboro and others spoke about the great things the Pioneer Mill had done for Maui, Lahaina resident Foster Ampong sat quietly, steadily leaning further and further forward in his metal folding chair. Sitting behind him, I could see that the people talking about cleaning up rats and how this building and that house needed to be saved, too, were clearly getting to him. Finally, he stood.

"Let's talk about the oligarchy," he said. The room got very quiet. "It was a bunch of guys who came into the islands . . . [They] brought in immigrants . . . water was stolen, land was stolen . . . The Pioneer Mill represents the oligarchy that nearly succeeded in [wiping out] the Hawaiian people." If Ampong was trying to start a debate, he didn't succeed. The meeting continued, as before. In this crowd, Ampong was definitely in the minority.

After the meeting, I asked him what he did for a living. "I'm my family genealogist," he said. "And I'm an advocate for independence." In fact, Ampong, who grew up in Lahaina, had numerous letters to the editor published in the *Honolulu Star-Bulletin,* among other papers, arguing against further commercial and residential development as well as a return to complete Hawaiian sovereignty. "I represent the [last] two percent of Native Hawaiians living today," he said, adding that he also had family ties to the plantation. His father had worked there for many years, just like Alboro.

"They talked about the stack, a museum—that's all they have to claim an identity," Ampong told me a couple days after the meeting. Even then, his blood was still up. "Most were immigrants brought in by the plantation. But I know where they're coming from. [But] no one looks at the bare truth of how many families were destroyed. All of us have been brought up to think that the [1893] overthrow was legitimate. I was ignorant for many years. It took my own research to uncover the facts. I wanted everyone to understand what they're advocating. It's the equivalent of me going to Auschwitz and saying that nothing happened. Everyone has acknowledged what devastation those camps caused. But here, they want to hold onto the mill as if it was a good thing."

I asked him what he sees whenever he looks at the mill.

"I see my family on my mother's side devastated," he said. "I see my great-grandfather, who had no choice but to succumb to the plantation to feed his family. The mill stole their water. I see my family dying. It's tough because people like the Alboros, they see it as life. The mill let them put their kids through college. I understand that."

Still, I couldn't shake the notion that Ampong was missing something important. He had used the hyperbolic Auschwitz metaphor, but hadn't followed it to its logical conclusion. A big part of the effort to make sure the world didn't forget the horrors of the Nazi death camp was keeping Auschwitz open to the public, as a kind of living reminder of the Holocaust.

But it didn't matter. The mill wasn't going to be saved. The KDC wanted to demolish it, and demolish it they did—not because they were ashamed of what went on there, but because of the enormous money the company could make on commercial and residential redevelopment of the land. Still, I fantasized about what could happen if there were a proper museum placed at the base of the smokestack, one dedicated to preserving the full, authentic history of both the mill and sugar production in Hawai'i. Yes, it was an economic engine that gave men like Alboro a decent chance to better their family's quality of life, but it had also been built without consent upon a fully functioning Hawai'i society—one that would never properly share in the profits it generated. Taking those steps could begin a new era in which locals could assert their culture and history in a meaningful way while the major sugar and land interests finally acknowledged the role they played in the destruction of the Hawaiian kingdom.

Of course it was never meant to be. Wriston had been coy about securing a caretaker for the smokestack, which I realized the second I saw George "Keoki" Freeland walk in the door at the town hall meeting. At the time, Freeland was executive director of the Lahaina Restoration Foundation. "Whether it's old or ancient, we'd like to see preservation of that site," Freeland said when asked about preserving the stack, then declined to elaborate. But Freeland had also been a former vice president and general manager of the Pioneer Mill Corporation, and there was no way he was going to let people like Ampong write the old mill's narrative.

Chapter 10

ROMANCE OF THE SKIES

If you've ever flown to Hawai'i out of Northern California, as I did on a couple occasions, then it's possible you flew over the grave of my cousin Albert. It's somewhere in the middle of the Pacific, midway between Hawai'i and California. No one really knows where it is because his body was never found. I was long established on Maui by the time I found all this out, though the fact that he died in the service of tourism will probably haunt me forever.

The crash of Pan Am Flight 7 on November 8, 1957, is one of the worst unsolved aviation disasters in American history. On that night, a four-engine Boeing B-377 Stratocruiser with the tail number 944 was carrying 44 people when it disappeared in the middle of the Pacific Ocean, approximately 1,000 miles northeast of O'ahu. It had left San Francisco earlier that day, bound for Honolulu. As far as anyone could tell, there had been no call for help and no indication whatsoever that anything had been wrong with the flight. The missing plane prompted the largest search effort in the Pacific since the disappearance of Amelia Earhart. Eventually, sailors pulled bits of wreckage, a few of the passengers' belongings and 19 bodies from the water. Albert Pinataro—the aircraft's flight engineer—wasn't among them.

Jean, Albert's sister, was 33 when the plane crashed, and the pain of his death never diminished in her life.

"I think he had a premonition that he was going to die," she told me in 2017 (Jean died in 2019, and the one good thing about my research into her brother's death was that I got to reconnect with her). "Not long before the crash, he wrote a letter to our Uncle Frank [my grandfather]—I think I'm going to cry. It said, 'If I die tomorrow, I'll die happy because I so love this job.'"

Unsolved air crashes are largely a thing of the past (the mysterious fate of Malaysian Airlines Flight 370, which vanished in 2014, is a notable exception), but Pan Am Flight 7 remains an open wound. It was a huge story across the nation when it happened, and the mystery of its fate fed all sorts of wild theories, including sabotage by a member of the crew, bombing by a deranged passenger, and, ultimately, assault by flying saucers. This isn't surprising. There's something unsettling about an aircraft and its passengers simply vanishing into the sky—especially one bound for paradise. But the crash gradually receded from the nation's collective memory, and the Stratocruiser itself, famous in its day, was soon forgotten after the introduction of jet airliners barely a year later.

In some ways, the story of what's known about the loss of Albert's plane is like a fantastic episode of the television documentary program *Air Disasters*. In each episode, an aircraft crashes (or suffers some sort of in-flight catastrophe but somehow lands), then investigators comb through debris, scrutinize the onboard Cockpit Voice Recorder (CVR) and Flight Data Recorder (FDR), work through hypotheses, settle on a cause and present their findings, which often end up making air travel safer for everyone.

But the loss of *Clipper Romance of the Skies* doesn't fit that formula. It crashed in the days before CVRs and FDRs. While authorities examined the available evidence for over a year, they never settled on a definitive cause. As a result, no one really learned anything from the crash—indeed, five more Stratocruisers were lost to accidents before the aircraft went out of service in the early 1960s.

When I set out to write about this, I combed through the old Civil Aeronautics Board (CAB—precursor to today's National Transportation Safety Board) report on the crash, photos of the wreckage itself, contemporary newspaper accounts, more recent magazine articles and Pan Am promotional materials. I thought that even though Albert was a cousin of mine, the fact that he'd died 15 years before I was born would make him a distant figure—just another name on the manifest. But I was wrong. In fact, by the end of my research, I even discovered a part of myself on that plane.

* * *

In August 1949—the same month that Pan Am first took delivery of *Romance of the Skies*—the magazine *FLYING* published a brief letter to the editor from Albert Pinataro, then living in Hollywood, California. Albert would have been about 18 at the time, and wrote the letter in response to a typographical error in a previous article about Lockheed's new Constellation, an airliner that ultimately proved far safer than the Stratocruiser.

"An item in 'Flat Spins' [June *FLYING*] stated: 'The Navy's giant Constellation is large enough to carry three railroad cars plus a standard passenger bus,'" Albert wrote. "If this is true I am sure Lockheed would like to know about it." The letter, which was the only one with his name on it that I could find in the magazine's archives, astonished me. Albert's use of gentle sarcasm struck me—my dad or uncle could have written the letter. Or me. "We are all that way!" my uncle had said when I told him about Albert's letter.

If you're wondering why Albert's last name differs slightly from mine, there's a simple explanation. In the early years of the twentieth century, two brothers—Pasquale and Frank Pignataro—emigrated to the United States from southern Italy. Upon arrival, Pasquale removed the "g" from his last name so it now spelled "Pinataro," to make the name closer to the true Italian pronunciation. But Frank left his last name as it was. Pasquale eventually had three children—Marie, who died in the early 1950s at age 30, Jean, and Albert. Frank had two sons—Frank Jr. (my dad) and Augustus (Gus).

Four of Pasquale and Frank's kids ended up in aviation. Both my father and his brother were aerospace engineers—for North American Aviation/Rockwell/Boeing and the U.S. Navy, respectively. Their cousins, Albert and his older sister Jean, had also made aviation a career.

Jean had been the first. After working as a sketch artist for Lockheed during World War II, she went to work for North American Aviation in the late 1940s as a technical artist, working on flight handbooks for test pilots. In the late 1960s she moved to the company's space division. There, in 1975, she designed the official crew patch for the famed Apollo-Soyuz mission in which American astronauts and Russian cosmonauts rendezvoused in Earth orbit.

"Albert learned how to fly before he learned to drive," Jean Pinataro told me. "[Before going to work for Pan Am] he went into the Air Force. He was in for four years. He worked as a mechanic. He was such a nice person, and was about to marry his girlfriend before the crash."

These were the days when cockpit crews were pretty much just white men—women who wanted to fly became stewardesses. The CAB report indicated that *Romance*'s flight crew on the night of the crash was thoroughly experienced and properly rested before the flight. Captain Gordon Brown had more than 11,000 hours in the air, though just 675 of those were in Stratocruisers. Albert Pinataro, the flight engineer, was the youngest and least experienced member of the crew.

"Flight Engineer Albert F. Pinataro, age 26, had been with PAWA since July 11, 1955," stated the CAB report on the crash. "Prior to employment with the company he had completed an aircraft maintenance course (9 months) at Glendale, California, Junior College and an aircraft and engine course (9 months) at Los Angeles City Aircraft School . . . His total flight time was 1,596:21 hours, all in Boeing 377 aircraft. Engineer Pinataro had 160 hours rest period prior to his duty assignment on Clipper 944 on November 8."

Researcher Gregg Herken, who dove deep into the records of the crash of Flight 7, told me Pinataro was taking night classes at the College of San Mateo in hopes of earning a promotion. My uncle, Gus Pignataro, also didn't remember much about him (he was pretty young when *Romance* crashed; my father, who knew Albert better and turned 18 just eight days after the crash, died in 2007).

"I only saw him a few times when I was very young," Gus told me. "I do remember that he wanted to do magic and he put together a complete one-man show. But I don't believe he ever performed before an audience. I do remember the crash. We first read it in the evening newspaper. They had a complete list of passengers and crew."

Because of my cousin Jean's background in aviation and space travel, she had a special appreciation for Albert's job. "He loved being a flight engineer," she told me. "It's a very complicated job. I've seen the flight engineer's panel [in a Boeing Stratocruiser]. It's about four feet wide, and stretches from the floor to the ceiling. It's covered with all kinds of switches and displays."

From pre-flight checks to engine shutdown after arrival, the flight engineer's job was to make sure the aircraft's power plants were working properly. On the Stratocruiser, the engineer sat in an office chair immediately behind the pilot and co-pilot, facing starboard. The introduction of computer-controlled flight systems in the 1980s rendered the flight engineer's job unnecessary, but in 1949, the Civilian Aviation Board mandated the position in all four-engine airliners to reduce the pilot's already considerable workload.

It was a difficult job that required meticulous attention. Nineteen months before the crash of *Romance of the Skies,* a Stratocruiser operated by Northwest Airlines took off from Seattle–Tacoma International Airport on its way to Portland, Chicago, and finally New York. Because of a single mistake made by the flight engineer before takeoff (though he told the pilot he would set the engine's "cowl flaps" for takeoff, he apparently never threw the switch), the Northwest Airlines plane was all but impossible to fly once it got into the air. The pilot chose to ditch in Puget Sound. Though all 38 passengers and crew survived the crash, four passengers and a flight attendant froze to death before they could be rescued.

* * *

At any given moment, the BBC series *City in the Sky* tells us, there are one million people in the air, carried by 100,000 flights every day. This wasn't the case 60 years ago, when air travel was still a luxury largely reserved for the wealthy.

This was the so-called "Golden Age of Air Travel," when airlines like Pan American were known around the world for style, comfort and safety. In fact, it was just fancy marketing. Air travel was expensive, slow and often dangerous.

Though sold to the public as the epitome of modern aeronautical engineering, the 42-ton Stratocruiser was already obsolete by 1957 (Boeing 707 jets, which could carry many more passengers at twice the speed, went into service with Pan Am just 11 months later). Introduced in 1949, the Stratocruiser was a civilian redesign of the B-29 Superfortress, the bomber that had dropped incendiary and nuclear weapons on Japanese cities during World War II. Pan Am, which wanted the plane because of its then-high speed and range, was Boeing's first customer.

"Biggest commercial landplane in the world, this impressive newcomer is years ahead in design, engineering and performance," read one 1949 Pan Am magazine advertisement. "This double-decked, luxury airliner will turn previously tiresome intercontinental journeys into brief flights of utmost comfort and convenience."

The phrase "brief flights" seems silly today. It took the Stratocruiser nine hours to fly from San Francisco to Honolulu, and other Pan Am routes were even longer. That's nine hours in a cramped cabin filled with cigarette smoke and constant engine vibrations. To make the journey even remotely desirable, Pan Am outfitted its Stratocruisers like cruise ships.

"At dinner time a seven-course meal is served from the ship's galley, the largest and most efficient flying kitchen in the world," boasts the 1950 Pan Am promotional film *The Double-Decked Strato "Clipper."* Though undoubtedly impressive at the time, the film today is a time capsule of post-war attitudes towards American wealth and the expected subservience of women. "Your dinner may be turned out with production-line efficiency, but it's a meal that any housewife would be proud to serve," the film states. "And you couldn't be more comfortable in your own dining room. With service like this, a trip by

Pan American Clipper is something more than the shortest distance between two points. It's more than the fastest, safest way to travel. It's a pleasure in itself."

Passenger seats reclined into sleeper beds, and leg room was an astonishing 60 inches (twice as much as found on today's 737s). There was even a bar downstairs—"a luxury that makes the plane flight part of your vacation," states the 1950 film. It's no wonder that Ian Fleming wrote in his James Bond novels (mostly published in the 1950s) that the Stratocruiser was 007's preferred method of travel.

But all that luxury came at considerable cost: the price of a ticket from San Francisco to Honolulu in 1957 was $300—the equivalent of about $2,600 today. What's more, Flight 7 was just the first leg of a Pan Am journey around the world. The total ticket cost of $1,600 pencils out to nearly $14,000 today.

The plane was a money-loser for Pan Am—though capable of carrying up to 100 passengers, many flights took off with less than half that number. And there was another problem with Stratocruisers—one that would cost Pan Am dearly in the coming decade. The aircraft's 3,500-horsepower engines, while quite powerful, were also extremely temperamental. Despite all Pan Am's marketing and public relations, the Stratocruiser wasn't a safe plane. Just 56 of the planes were built, and in its 14 years in commercial service, 10 were destroyed in accidents—nearly 18 percent of the entire production run. Of those accidents, five were due to engine or propeller problems. Overspeeding or runaway props, which plagued Stratocruiser flights especially in the aircraft's early years, posed a special danger to the aircraft and its passengers and crew.

"[T]here was a danger that it would fly apart and pieces would penetrate the fuselage," researchers Gregg Herken and Ken Fortenberry wrote in a 2004 *Air & Space* article. "[A] runaway could occur virtually without warning, and left the pilots only seconds to react."

In fact, just a year prior to the crash of *Romance of the Skies,* the Pan Am clipper *Sovereign of the Skies* experienced a runaway prop while trying to fly to Hawai'i. *Sovereign*'s pilot was able to ditch in daylight close to the Coast Guard weather ship *Pontchartrain,* which rescued all 31 passengers and crew members.

Though the CAB's crash report stated that *Romance of the Skies* had never experienced any propeller overspeeding in its career, Herken and Fortenberry found evidence that indicated otherwise. In fact, former Pan Am pilot Clancy Mead told them that he'd dealt with a runaway prop while trying to fly *Romance of the Skies* to Hawai'i just six months before its crash. "Unable to feather the prop on the no. 3 engine [the engine closest to the fuselage on the aircraft's starboard wing], and losing altitude at a rate of 100 feet per minute—even with the remaining engines at rated power—Mead turned 944 and headed back to San Francisco," Herken and Fortenberry wrote in 2004. "He estimated *Romance* cleared the mountains along the coast by only 500 feet. Luckily, he was able to set the airplane down safely at the airport."

* * *

According to a November 10, 1957, *Honolulu Star-Bulletin* article, there was just one Hawai'i resident on Pan Am Flight 7—Specialist Third Class David A. Hill, 21, a soldier stationed at Schofield Barracks on O'ahu. There were also two former Hawai'i residents on the manifest—Louis Rodrigues, 53, formerly of Pu'unene, and Frederick Choy, 26, whose parents still resided in Honolulu. None of their bodies were recovered.

The day after *Romance* disappeared, the *Oakland Tribune* reported that the loss of the plane was shocking because "the 2,400-mile San Francisco–Honolulu trip is considered one of the safest runs in the world." According to the paper, "only four persons have lost their lives in peacetime accidents between the two points." It was an ironic statement: those four deaths happened just two years earlier, when another Pan Am Stratocruiser, the *Clipper United States,* ditched in the ocean off Portland, Oregon, after a propeller tore loose in flight. Nineteen of the 23 people aboard survived.

The effort to find the wreck of *Romance of the Skies* was "one of the greatest air and sea searches in Pacific Ocean history," according to the *Tribune*. It included the weather ship *Minnetonka,* two Coast Guard cutters, the submarines *Cusk* and *Carbonero,* various tankers and freighters, the passenger liner *Matsonia* and more than a dozen patrol planes. The navy coordinated everything from the aircraft carrier *Philippine Sea,* which was necessary because the search area covered more than 100,000 square miles.

For four days, no one saw a trace of the missing plane. Then, on November 14, 1957, spotters on a search aircraft saw debris—and bodies—spread out over the 30-square-mile area. "The first body recovered earlier today from the sea was that of a man wearing dark clothing and a yellow life jacket," *Los Angeles Times* reporter Deke Houlgate, who had wrangled himself a spot on the *Philippine Sea,* reported on November 14. "The body was without shoes as were many of the others recovered later. All the bodies had external injuries and multiple fractures. Cause of death was considered to be from extensive injuries rather than exposure or drowning."

In fact, the CAB later reported that drowning was "probably" the cause of death for 10 of the recovered bodies. "Further, the lack of extensive crash-induced mutilation, together with the general condition of the bodies, suggested that the water impact, although severe, was not sufficiently great to cause complete disintegration of the aircraft," the CAB crash report noted. Eventually, sailors pulled 19 bodies from the sea. According to Houlgate, two of the bodies wore wristwatches stopped at 7:25, while a third wore one that was stopped at 5:25 (apparently adjusted for Hawai'i time). The CAB report later reported these times as "26 and 27 minutes past the hour" and settled on 5:27 p.m. Hawai'i time as the approximate time of the crash.

Houlgate reported that the debris from *Romance of the Skies* filled 14 cardboard boxes and two wooden crates. His list of what sailors recovered includes the following:

"A ladies washroom door with printing in English and some Oriental language."

"The snapshot of a man."

"A white toy dog made of fabric with a ribbon around its neck."

"An orange squeezer."

"A Christmas card reading 'Greetings from our house to your house' with the picture of a baby."

CAB investigators had a difficult, if not impossible, task ahead of them. There were no survivors, and the flight crew hadn't radioed for help—or if they did, no one heard it. Sailors had only recovered a tiny portion of the aircraft, and what debris they did pull out of the water was basically just bits of twisted metal.

CAB's final report on the crash, issued on January 20, 1959, revealed a number of important clues into the fate of *Romance,* but no firm answers. The stopped wristwatches indicated that the plane had plunged into the sea a little more than 20 minutes after the flight crew had radioed their last position report. The weather the night of the crash had been clear, and other pilots had reported calm seas. Aircraft maintenance records showed "nothing that could be related directly to the accident."

The fact that 14 of the 19 recovered bodies wore life jackets meant the passengers and crew were prepared for a ditching. Though some of the wreckage was damaged by fire, all the burn marks were above the waterline, which meant any fire occurred after the aircraft hit the ocean. Carbon monoxide was found in many of the bodies that had been recovered, but investigators later concluded it was most likely a result of prolonged exposure to the elements.

As to whether the crew of *Romance* had called for help, the CAB report could make no determination. Though there were tapes of "previously unknown transmissions which were extremely weak," they were "subject to varied and conflicting interpretation." Ultimately, the CAB simply had no explanation for the loss of *Romance*. "The Board has insufficient tangible evidence at this time to determine the cause of the accident," the report concluded.

Given the way in which *Romance of the Skies* crashed, without a definite call for help or clear explanation, it's perhaps inevitable that science fiction would soon bleed into media accounts of the crash. In fact, the *Philippine Sea* was still collecting debris from the *Romance of the Skies* when the first nonsense surrounding the crash started appearing in papers.

After first agreeing that the most likely explanation for the crash was either sabotage or mechanical failure, *Honolulu Star-Bulletin* Managing Editor William H. Ewing then wrote in a November 13, 1957, column that, "Interestingly enough, there are men who fly for a living who do not rule out the space ship theory—that a strange craft able to knock out electrical circuits, as was reported in last week's rash of flying saucer stories—could have been responsible."

Even in the 1950s, this was sensationalist, exploitative garbage, though it's true some of those participating in the search sometimes offered wild, irresponsible theories about what brought the plane down. On November 15, 1957, the *Fresno Bee* reported that "a navy officer who has been participating in the search from Pearl Harbor" listed three possible explanations for the loss of the plane: "There could have been a fire, a propeller could have flown off, or a meteor could have hit the plane."

In no time at all, the flying saucer community of the late 1950s—which was considerable—had adopted the crash of Pan Am Flight 7 as just more evidence that aliens were racing across our skies. In 1958, a guy named Reinhold Schmidt even started publishing stories saying that during an alien abduction, his captors had asked him a number of questions, including if he knew what the *Romance of the Skies* had been carrying in its hold when it crashed. *Romance* is also included in George D. Fawcett's 1961 book, *The Flying Saucers Are Hostile!*, which stated, without any evidence, that "UFOs had been reported in the vicinity" of the crash.

Perhaps the most callous manipulation of the *Romance* crash dealt not with flying saucers but with some recovered mail the plane had been carrying. On December 4, 1957, the *Honolulu Star-Bulletin* reported not only that such mail might be valuable, but offered tips on how to maximize its selling price.

"Here's a tip to those who receive this type of mail," H.E. Bauer wrote. "Keep the cover as you receive it; that is, remove the letter without damaging the envelope more than it already its. The postage stamp will probably be missing. Don't worry about that but be sure to leave the postmark intact. Don't 'monkey' with it."

* * *

We live in a world where commercial flying is routine, even boring. But there's also a fact about air travel that, if you start thinking about it—especially once you get in the air—you'll start to feel very weird. When you take your seat, very often you don't have any idea who the person is sitting next to you. I kept thinking about this while reading the latest research into the fate of Pan Am Flight 7.

As far as factual explanations for the loss of *Romance of the Skies,* the CAB report stood pretty much alone for more than four decades. Then in 2004, two independent researchers—Gregg Herken and Ken Fortenberry—published a story in the magazine *Air & Space* that provided a trove of new information on the crash. Like me, both men have personal ties to members of *Romance*'s crew: Flight Attendant Marie McGrath had been one of Herken's favorite substitute teachers, and navigator William Fortenberry was Ken's father. Neither body was ever found.

In addition to reporting Clancy Mead's previous problems with an overspeeding prop on *Romance,* they also identified two possible suspects who might have sabotaged the aircraft for criminal reasons. The first, Eugene Crosthwaite, was the 46-year-old purser on the flight. He was Pan Am's chief suspect. "Crosthwaite once bragged that he had deliberately dropped a meal on the galley floor before serving it to an unsuspecting captain, who he felt had insulted him," Herken and Fortenberry wrote. "Furthermore, Crosthwaite blamed Pan Am for several misfortunes, including the tuberculosis he'd contracted in Shanghai before the war, while serving as a purser on the airline's flying boats."

Despondent over the death of his wife, Crosthwaite had amended his will the morning of the last flight of *Romance.* "Pan Am considered the changed will a smoking gun," the authors wrote. But then a new suspect appeared.

"William Harrison Payne, 41, listed as a passenger on *Romance of the Skies,* was reportedly on his way to Hawai'i to collect an overdue debt," they wrote. "Among the more curious details about Payne—whose body was not recovered—was the fact that the purported debt amounted to less than the price of the one-way ticket to Honolulu he had purchased." He'd taken out three insurance policies on himself before the flight—including one that paid double in the event of accidental death—and had been a demolitions expert in the Navy (Pan Am even conceded that it was possible Payne had never boarded *Romance of the Skies*).

It wasn't until 2014, when Herken and Fortenberry finally gained access to the Pan Am archives at the University of Miami's Special Collections Library, that a clearer explanation of the crash emerged. Though the case is by no means closed, the researchers were able to find that it was likely *Romance* did call for help. They also found that Pan Am and the CAB itself had colluded to whitewash the airline's poor record of maintaining their Stratocruiser fleet. "One of the most dramatic moments of the [CAB investigation] hearings had been the testimony of Phil Ice, president of the Transport Workers Union's Local 505, whose members maintained Pan American's fleet of aircraft in San Francisco," the authors wrote in their January 2017 *Air & Space* article, "What Happened to Pan Am Flight 7?" "Ice bemoaned a 'drastic curtailment of inspection personnel' by Pan Am, resulting in 'dangerous deficiencies in inspection and maintenance.'"

CAB had even sent its own inspectors to Pan Am's maintenance shop. "They reported to their superiors: 'Inspection and/or quality control in the engine overhaul is not adequate," Herken and Fortenberry wrote. "'Maintenance practices are questionable.'"

It got worse. "The maintenance logs entered into evidence at the hearings told another troubling tale," the authors wrote. "In the weeks before the crash, 944's engines had experienced 'a constant fluctuation' in oil pressure, leaks from the turbochargers, and persistent cooling problems."

This is damning evidence that makes a mockery of the CAB report's finding that *Romance*'s maintenance records held "nothing that could be directly related to the accident." So was the May 1958 letter from a Pan Am attorney to a CAB official, calling on the board to "withhold the maintenance report from the public record," that Herken and Fortenberry found. Today, the FAA—which both regulates and promotes the airline industry—and the NTSB are separate agencies. But back in 1958, the CAB was responsible for everything—a huge conflict of interest.

"Ultimately, what brought down *Romance of the Skies* was human fallibility," Herken and Fortenberry wrote. "A propulsion technology had reached its limits. A government agency had become cozy with the companies it was meant to police. And an airline, in its rush to enter the jet age, had decided to cut corners, ignoring the risk to passengers and crew."

* * *

In 2020, Fortenberry published his own book on Flight 7, pinning the blame for the crash on Crosthwaite. But his work offered little conclusive evidence beyond what he and Herken had already reported. In fact, the whole book seemed forced, almost arbitrary, and did not refute any of the authors' earlier conclusions on Boeing maintenance practices and collusion with the CAB.

In any case, reading that letter to the editors of *FLYING* that Albert had written when he was barely an adult forced me to think about something new. I had always known that I got my sense of humor from my dad, but never really considered where he got it. That his father had it too makes sense, but here was evidence that my grandfather's brother had it as well—and had passed it onto someone who had died long before I was ever born. If that were true, then where had my grandfather and his brother gotten their sense of humor? They had left Italy in the early years of the twentieth century—were there relatives of mine over there right now, thinking and cracking wise in eerily similar ways to me? And how far back do other parts of my personality—my way of thinking, reasoning, feeling—date back?

I had never anticipated that Albert and I might think in similar ways—might react to events in similar ways. This revelation yanked me out of the comfortable, cushioned chair at my desk and dropped me into the cockpit of *Romance of the Skies*. Flying at 10,000 feet or so, passing the point of no return on what would be its last flight, what would I have done when whatever happened actually happened?

I'd like to think I would have fallen back on my training, concentrated on my job and done everything possible to ensure that the passengers seated behind me had the greatest possible chances at survival, and that Albert did the same. I don't know, of course, and will likely never know. Sometimes, all we have are questions with no answers.

Chapter 11

KĀʻANAPALI

The selling of Maui to tourists and land speculators really took off in the early 1960s with the introduction of jet airlines, which had begun replacing old propeller planes like the *Romance of the Skies* in 1957. American Factors (later shortened to Amfac) was one of Hawaiʻi's "Big Five" landowners. Since 1849, the company had farmed sugarcane, an inherently filthy industry that blackened the skies above Hawaiʻi with soot and smoke. At its peak, Amfac owned 60,000 acres of the state. But by the early '60s, tourism promised far more profits than cane fields ever could. So Amfac, run largely, if not exclusively, by white men, began developing its holdings just north of Lahaina, on Maui's leeward coast, where warm morning sun gives way to refreshing late afternoon rain nearly 12 months out of the year.

In 1962, the Royal Lahaina Resort opened. Its bungalows held 186 rooms, but it also offered a massive 18-hole golf course designed by the famous architect Robert Trent Jones. A year later, the sprawling 212-room Sheraton Maui Resort opened atop Black Rock, an environmental and cultural cataclysm I doubt would happen today. Known to the Kānaka Maoli as Puʻu Kekaʻa, Black Rock was formed by lava nearly 600,000 years ago. To them, it was an immensely important place, where the spirits of the dead leaped from the Earth. If there was any Hawaiian opposition to the hotel's construction, it didn't make it into the papers—I found more in the microfilmed pages of the old *Honolulu Advertiser* about the difficulties in getting palm trees to grow atop Black Rock (water drained into the lava before feeding the tree) than I did on indigenous opposition to the new resort.

A year after the Sheraton opened, in 1964, Amfac released a 20-minute film, simply titled *Kaanapali*. The audience was rich white people, who are about the only people to appear in it. Kāʻanapali is "the Polynesian Riviera," "the new queen of resorts" and "a builder's dream," according to the film. "Land that was once trod by kings is today an international playground," says the narrator over shots of Kāʻanapali from the air, as if from one of the prop planes carrying visitors that often landed at the tiny air strip at nearby Kahekili Beach (today colloquially known as "Airport Beach"). At Kāʻanapali, the narrator advised, "sophistication meets nature, and nature lends itself to man." Though marketed as a wonderland of Hawaiʻi, the Kāʻanapali resorts offered amenities often found in the continental United States. Indeed, the film showed a suit-and-tie-clad guy who bore more than a casual resemblance to Spiro Agnew partaking in "ribs, roasts, chops and steaks" in the Royal Lahaina dining room. The narrator embraced this odd paradox, saying the resorts were "American in service, native in enjoyment." What that meant in practical terms is what we call settler colonialism today: "natives" lighting torches on Black Rock at sunset (which is still done today) was merely a signal for "cocktail time," while guys taking a hatchet to rare black coral reefs offshore was necessary to make more "necklaces, earrings and cufflinks."

Most laughable was the 1964 narrator's assertion that even though more resorts would follow the Royal Lahaina and Sheraton, Kāʻanapali's "guardians" would "always keep the sands open and uncrowded." Since the Johnson Administration, this has only been true during the first year of the COVID-19 pandemic, when tourist flights to Hawaiʻi went to zero—a catastrophe for the local economy, but residents enjoyed wide open Kāʻanapali Beach as few had since Captain Cook's arrival in the state.

Residential access to Kāʻanapali, though mandated by state law, which ensures public access to all the shoreline in the state, has never been easy. Even today, residents who want to surf, fish or just jump in the water at Kāʻanapali Beach can expect a difficult journey when trying to find a parking place. The lots that do cater to the public tend to be cramped and scattered around the various resorts. It used to be even worse, with signage minimal or simply nonexistent. Other times, public parking lots were loaded with signs listing restrictions on when people can park there—restrictions that were, in fact, not legal.

For decades, Randy Draper, who lived in nearby Nāpili, worked hard to change that. A longtime West Maui resident, he'd been running on Kāʻanapali Beach since there were just three hotels there. He remembered the place before the paved beach paths and tens of thousands of visiting tourists that now lay on the sand and snorkeled in the water every day. He also understood better than most people how public access to the beach, once easy decades earlier, was now being constricted by the resorts. State law mandated public beach access, but they'd been getting away with treating Kāʻanapali Beach as their private property, and Draper was sick of it.

"After the county gave out the [resort] permits, nothing was checked," Draper told me not long after I moved to Maui. "They let guests and employees park in them. So it's gonna take some time for it to work itself out."

Draper—a retired boat captain—knew all about this because he'd been agitating for greater public beach parking access for the last 50 years. That's right—for pretty much the entire time there have been resorts at Kāʻanapali, Draper's been calling for more parking.

But in 2016, after many decades, Draper was a happy man. That's because the Maui County Planning Department finally got serious about enforcing the public beach access parking requirements that were part of each resort's development permit. After months spent researching the resorts' original permits, Deputy Planning Director Michele Chouteau McLean (the same Michele McLean who, as an agent of West Maui Land Co., had helped orchestrate the PR campaign for Puʻunoa back in Olowalu years prior) mailed letters to all the Kāʻanapali resorts in early March of that year detailing their compliance—or noncompliance—with the parking regulations.

"It's because I made 'em do it," Draper said proudly when I asked him why all this was happening now. "[Attorney] Lance Collins helped me get the county to look at the permits." McLean confirmed that she worked "back and forth" with Draper on this. "It took a while to research," she said. "We had to spend time pulling the files." In the county's research, two issues became clear: not all resorts were providing the required number of public parking spaces, while others had put up signs warning those parking there against using the spaces at night. In fact, McLean confirmed, there are no time restrictions on public access beach parking in Kāʻanapali.

McLean sent out letters to six Kāʻanapali resorts, as well as Whaler's Village. According to the letters, which I obtained, the majority of resorts were providing the required number of spaces. But two—the Westin Maui Resort & Spa and Marriott's Maui Ocean Club—were not. "A recent site visit confirmed that the Westin is providing only 28 of the required 30 parking spaces, situated facing the building (facing away from Whaler's Village)," McLean wrote to Westin officials. "You must provide two additional spaces to comply with the requirement of 30 spaces."

Westin Public Relations Director Sumithra Balraj, one of the few resort officials who agreed to talk to me on the issue, insisted that the resort was providing the required number of spaces. "The Westin Maui Resort & Spa is offering 30 parking spaces for public beach access without any time restrictions," Balraj said in an email to me. "We had informed the county office of our 30 allocated parking spaces and as such, they should have this updated information."

Far more problematic, though, was the situation at the Marriott. In fact, McLean herself said in her email to Draper that she was "curious" as to how the Marriott would deal with their problem. That's because the Marriott was providing just 10 of the 30 required public beach access parking spaces. Though the Marriott's own people promised to provide 35 parking spots, county officials found that just a third were actually in existence.

In fact, I didn't know the Marriott provided any public parking spaces until I walked around the property while researching for this story. But sure enough, I found the 10 spaces McLean mentioned in her letter, tucked away at the south end of the property. There was a sign labeling them as public, but it was buried in trees and completely invisible from someone driving by just a few yards away. Given the parking situation at the Marriott, it was unclear to me where the resort would put another 20 spaces.

The Planning Department also found that two resorts—the Kāʻanapali Aliʻi and the Kāʻanapali Beach Hotel (KBH)—had placed signs that unlawfully told the public they couldn't park there at night. What's more, the Kāʻanapali Aliʻi also routinely chained up its lot at night, potentially forcing those who'd parked there past the "closing time" to get their car out of an impound lot. That infuriated Draper.

"The Aliʻi's had it locked up for 20, 30 years," Draper said. "The public should be able to go to any beach parking lot and then go fishing without getting their car impounded."

County planning inspectors also apparently found problematic signage at the KBH. "[S]ome of the spaces are not identified at the entrance of each space," McLean wrote in a letter to KBH General Manager Mike White. "They are each marked with a sign that is hung on the fence at the end of each space; some are appropriately marked on the pavement, while others have faded 'valet parking' marked on the pavement. This must be corrected so that each space is identified at the entrance (i.e., marked on the pavement for public beach parking)."

The county's including of the KBH in this really fascinated me because, at the time, White (not to be confused with the Mike White who is the showrunner for the HBO series *The White Lotus*) was also the chairman of the Maui County Council and the county's most powerful foe of McLean's boss, Maui

Mayor Alan Arakawa. He'd run the KBH since the mid-1980s, and was himself a former state legislator. He was a smart, experienced and dedicated friend to Maui's tourist industry, which is probably how KBH was able to get away with billing itself as the "most Hawaiian" hotel in the state.

But it seemed that some night restrictions may have been if not completely legal, then at least officially allowed. I discovered this when looking at the then-new Hyatt Residence Club, located between the Hyatt Regency and the Marriott Maui Ocean Club, which opened in late 2014. That resort had a public beach access parking lot with 20 stalls (one of which was designated ADA-accessible) that sat next to the inadequate Marriott's 10-space lot. Though McLean's letter to the Hyatt did not mention inspectors finding any time restriction signs on the property's 74 parking spaces, my own visit to the resort found that each space in this particular lot was marked with a sign warning against parking there between 8pm and 6am.

Jim Cooper, the Residence Club's general manager, insisted that his resort was in compliance and those restrictions were legal. "We have to follow the rules very carefully," he said. "And we've had every inspector in the world here over the last two years."

In response, McLean told me that it was "unclear" whether the time restrictions on those 20 spaces were permitted. She said there had been "discussions" in the past about allowing that particular resort to restrict public beach parking access at night to make it easier for delivery trucks to get in and out (the lot sits in front of the Residence Club parking garage). But McLean also said her inspectors were unable to find any documentary evidence that those discussions led to official approvals.

In all of her correspondence, McLean said her department would "continue to monitor compliance" and called on the resorts to step up enforcement. "[W]e would appreciate your efforts to ensure that the public beach parking is truly being used by the public and not by any hotel vendors, employees or parking valets," she wrote. "[W]hile we understand that enforcement in this regard is a challenge, we expect reasonable effort." Later, I asked McLean what she meant exactly by "reasonable effort."

"It's hard to define," she said. "It's really hard to do—we know, because we do enforcement. But I think that when they realize the county is involved, they'll make an effort."

Draper was enough of a realist to know that they probably wouldn't. For that reason, he wanted the public to be extra vigilant—a necessity he'd learned in the decades he'd spent trying to get resorts to do something simple like stop restricting beach access to residents. "It's basically going to be enforced by the public," Draper said. "People need to be conscious of their environment there. If they're not watching closely, it can get taken away from them."

Two years later, Mike White struck back and attempted to undo all the work Draper had done.

On January 9, 2018, the County Council's Parks, Recreation, Energy, and Legal Affairs (PRL) Committee held an utterly insulting and useless meeting on a new bill White proposed on the issue. I say insulting because the bill would have allowed resorts (like the Kāʻanapali Beach Hotel, where White was still working as general manager, which is mandated by the county to provide 10 public access beach parking spots) to prohibit public beach access parking between 9:00 p.m. and 6:00 a.m. And I say useless because Councilmember Don Guzman, the chair of the PRL Committee, deferred any committee discussion on the bill because White never showed up to the meeting. But the committee still heard public testimony on the bill, and I can sum it all up with just one word: Outrage.

"This is an anti-community bill," former Councilmember Wayne Nishiki testified. "Throw this bill away. It makes no sense to me why this was even conceived."

Wayne's daughter Kai, who was also an activist, was just as angry. "Where's Mike White?" she asked at the start of her testimony. "This is his bill, right? Some shameful." Later, she called his bill "a clear conflict of interest."

Councilmember Yuki Lei Sugimura seemed insulted by Kai Nishiki's testimony, and even challenged her on her conflict-of-interest allegations. After asking her if she'd provided a Tax Map Key proving that White's bill affected the KBH, Sugimura told Kai Nishiki she was merely "assuming" that the bill dealt with that resort.

"No, I'm not," Kai Nishiki countered, before explaining how it's public knowledge that the Planning Department requires the resorts, including the KBH, to provide public beach access parking.

"I'll ask the questions," Sugimura replied, before ending her questioning.

Later, Councilmember Kelly King asked Kai Nishiki if the public beach access parking spots are adequately labeled.

"It's kind of a problem," she responded. "Why do I, a single mom, have to go enforce public parking? That's not my job."

Though Guzman deferred the bill to a later meeting, it never appeared again on a committee agenda. In April of that year, White announced that he would retire from the County Council when his current term ended later that year. "In early 2019, my responsibilities to the owners of the hotel will significantly increase, making it difficult to dedicate the necessary time to both roles," he said in a statement to supporters. White's priorities in life surprised few who'd watched his work on the council through the years.

Chapter 12

RACISM

My first stint as *MauiTime* editor ended in the spring of 2008. My father had died a few months prior. I was 36 years old, and for the first time in my life, pretty much alone in life. I took some of the money my sister (who lived in Texas) and I split from the sale of the house we grew up in, and resigned from *MauiTime*. My thought was that I would live as a freelance writer on Maui, writing only what I wanted to write. But the economy was lousy, and few magazines focusing on Hawaiʻi were interested in my story pitches. I lasted a year, then left Maui entirely for Sacramento, California. I didn't really know anyone there, but decided I wanted to cover the state capital for someone. I found a place to live, then started writing freelanced stories for the local alt weekly there, the *Sacramento News & Review*. Eventually I got a job as a reporter for a new journalism startup funded by a libertarian think tank. For about a year, I wrote a variety of pieces, long and short, on the state government. I did some good work there, but my heart wasn't in it.

I also missed Maui. It didn't help when one day in early November 2010, I randomly called up *The Maui News* website on my phone to see what was happening on the island, only to find a story about how my friend Gianna had died a couple nights prior. She had apparently fallen asleep at the wheel while driving home from a late-night party. Gianna was originally from Florida, and like many mainlanders who moved to Maui, had done so for the surfing and climate. But while many stayed just a year, eventually returning to where they came from, Gianna had stayed. She also found creative inspiration. She had written a few stories for *MauiTime,* and later took over a small cafe in Lahaina, which functioned as both a gathering place for friends and an art studio for herself. When she secured a spot for some of her ocean-themed paintings in a

Front Street art gallery, I considered buying one, but declined because of the price. I had last talked to her a few days before I moved off island, but hadn't kept in touch. Now I was lying on a friend's bed, staring at a news story that matter-of-factly quoted the Maui Police describing the time and place of her death. Like many who've died on Maui's roads, Gianna got a crude cross with her name painted on it, tacked up to the huge tree her car had hit by some of her friends.

In early 2011, I resigned again, and once again started freelancing. I was a few months into it when Tommy Russo, still the publisher of *Maui Time,* called me. He said the guy who'd replaced me as editor was resigning and moving back to California with his family. Then he asked if I'd like to come back.

It wasn't a straightforward decision. I had a girlfriend, Angie, now, and I'd been away from Maui for two years. The salary was exactly where I'd left it—$42,000 a year. Still, I liked the idea of returning. I asked Angie, and she agreed to go with me, even though it was unlikely she'd find any work commensurate with her current job as an analyst with the state government. So in June of that year, I put my car back on a boat for Maui.

The island was almost exactly as I'd left it. Many of the same officials were still in the county, so the learning curve was practically nonexistent. But the confidence I had returning to my old job wasn't earned. I was experienced in editing and news writing, certainly, but my understanding of Maui's demographics wasn't nuanced. See, for many transplants, living happily in Hawai'i requires amnesia, either willful or born of ignorance. You have to ignore a lot, or simply refuse to accept a lot, in order to function with any degree of optimism. I was this way for a long time—far too long, to be honest. Sure, I was a progressive journalist, radical even in some ways, but terribly ignorant about issues of racism and misogyny. I can still recall when that changed.

I'd been back at *Maui Time* for about a year or two, and I wrote a story on a small nonprofit that cared for elderly people suffering from dementia. Though I had taken what I thought were great pains in showing care to the patients, I had identified one as "Asian," while not identifying the race of anyone else in the facility. It had never occurred to me, in all my previous years working as a journalist, that such an act could be racist. Yet it was—I was acting as though whites were the default race in society and othering those who weren't. But when a reader sent me an anonymous email pointing this out and saying what I had done was racist, I reacted exactly like most white males unused to questioning their own privileges and assumptions do—poorly. I quickly wrote back, denying that I was in any way a racist and saying the email was unfair.

But over the next few days, I found myself obsessing about the email. If I was so certain that I wasn't a racist, then why had someone taken the time to say that I was? I began reading what I could on racism, seeking out what I could. In no time at all I saw that, yup, what I did was racist—clearly so, in fact.

I began to read bell hooks, James Baldwin, and Claudia Rankine. Studies of racism inevitably led me to sexism, and I devoured more books and articles by Rebecca Solnit, Rebecca Traister, Charlotte Shane, Moira Donegan and others. The works of Kate Manne, a philosopher at Cornell University, on misogyny and entitlement, were especially helpful. On Twitter, I began to seek out Hawaiian and indigenous activists—just to observe, never to debate. I started following Daniel Heath Justice, Terese Mailhot, and in Hawai'i, University of Hawai'i Maui College Hawaiian Studies Professor Kaleikoa Ka'eo, Hawai'i Commission on the Status of Women Executive Director Khara Jabola-Carolus, and many others. Often, these activists harshly denounced the actions of the U.S. government—and white men in particular. But instead of becoming defensive, I found myself wanting to know more. Slowly, I started to learn—or rather, unlearn—what I'd already spent a lifetime learning. Any feeling of hurt pride I'd felt quickly gave way to real horror—what damage had my ignorance and arrogance done throughout my previous decades as a journalist? Had my thoughtlessness been hurting some of the very people I was trying to assist?

To be clear, a great deal of bad writing on Hawai'i and racism has and continues to flow from the mainstream media. In 1965, *The New York Times* published an article titled "Multi-Racial Hawai'i Is Without Race Problem." The deck alone is astonishingly bad: "People Grow Up 'Color Blind' Because Early Settlers Needed Natives in Order to Exist." In fact, nearly every word of the headline and deck are so wrong as to constitute racist propaganda.

"Hawai'i also escaped the typical patterns of colonialization," states the article. "No western power considered it important enough to take over. And the plantation system, which has usually been based on domination of one racial group by another, never developed that way here."

Again, this is beyond nonsense. Hawai'i had literally been a "territory" of the United States just six years prior to this story being published. The United States, the richest "western power" of the twentieth century, took over Hawai'i in 1898 and made it officially a colony. By then, the sugar interests had long imposed a plantation system on Hawai'i in which white overseers sat at the top and every other ethnic group (Japanese, Chinese, Portuguese, Filipinos, and Hawaiians) lived in separate "camps"—though to be clear, former camp residents even into the early 2000s still expressed fond memories for their youths in such conditions. During a talk at the Ritz-Carlton in late 2003, Wes Nohara, then the manager of the Maui Pineapple Company, remembered trying to play football on a triangle field or swinging a toy jet attached to surgical tubing above his head at the old Honolua Plantation camps, which occupied the land prior to the resort's construction. "There was lots of prejudice, but there's that everywhere," Nohara said.

The need for journalists from outside the state—especially at the *New York Times*—to remanufacture Hawai'i into a racism-free paradise continues to the present day. In March 2017, the *Times* published a travel story by Wells Tower titled "The Hawai'i Cure: A first trip to the island, in a desperate bid to escape the news." Such articles are predicated on the all-too-common view that Hawai'i is a magical refuge from the rest of the world, where "the news" doesn't happen. "Can it be true?" Tower asked. "The aloha spirit is real? Paradise on earth? An Eden of happy Americans moated from our national ravages of malevolence, contempt, uncertainty and fear?" Writing like this reinforces the view, conscious or subconscious, in tourists' minds that all of Hawai'i is a theme park, built and maintained for their enjoyment. Tower visits a couple islands in the chain, but views everything through the lens of a slightly bemused visitor, commenting on the availability of parking and whether he'll be able to "poke lava with a stick" as though Hawai'i and its residents have nothing to offer but amusements for sale.

Just two years later, an opinion piece in—you guessed it—*The New York Times* asks readers, "Want to Be Less Racist? Move to Hawai'i." To be fair, the piece is a far more nuanced look at racism than the asinine headline advertises, but it's still predicated on the view that racism itself is different in Hawai'i.

It. Is. Not.

Racism led to the overthrow of the Hawaiian Kingdom, the imposition of industrialized sugar plantations and the current state economy based overwhelmingly on tourism. It has been in Hawai'i since Captain Cook's visit (which ended with the good captain's head on a stick) and has been present in the islands ever since. I've already talked about the disproportionate jailing of Native Hawaiians, but there are other forms of racism in the state as well. Today, white and ethnic Japanese residents of Hawai'i sit atop the political and economic pyramid, while everyone else toils, and the myriad other groups who call the state home try to make do with scraps, according to a well-researched 2021 *National Geographic* piece by Imani Altemus-Williams and Marie Eriel Hobro—a rare example of a mainstream publication reporting responsibly about Hawai'i.

"Native Hawaiians have among the highest poverty rates on the islands and make up some 20 percent of Hawai'i's houseless population," the authors state. "Samoans, Tongans, and Filipinos struggle with low per capita incomes, while more than half of Hawai'i's Marshallese population are impoverished."

Micronesian residents catch racist hell from nearly everyone else in Hawai'i, study after study shows. "[O]verall, 1 in 4 Micronesians in the sample of 517 Micronesians in Hawai'i reported that they had experienced some type of biased behavior toward them because they are Micronesian," according to a survey conducted by the University of Hawai'i at Mānoa Myron B. Thompson School of Social Work in 2017 and 2018. Another study, released by the Hawai'i Scholars for Education and Social Justice in 2022, found that just half of Micronesian students who entered the ninth grade between 2013 and 2018 actually graduated from high school, according to *Honolulu Civil Beat*. That study also determined that racism towards the Micronesian students came not merely from classmates, but also from teachers and school officials.

It's not that Hawai'i is paradise lost, but that it was never paradise to begin with.

Chapter 13

SEWAGE

In the spring of 2020, the U.S. Supreme Court, so often the source of misery in recent years for people who believe in civil rights and environmental protection, issued a rare ruling that actually made environmentalists breathe a bit easier. In a 6–3 decision, the court found that the County of Maui could not sidestep the Clean Water Act by pumping sewage into the groundwater—without a federal permit. For years, the county's West Maui sewage treatment plant, located just north of Kā'anapali, had injected millions of gallons of treated sewage into the ground. The county's reasoning was that the Clean Water Act only covered pollution entering navigable waters. A variety of environmental organizations had opposed this, saying the sewage the county was pumping into the ground was definitely finding its way from the water table into the ocean. The county (of course) ignored them, which culminated in their filing a federal lawsuit against the county in 2012. The Trump Administration eventually got on board, siding with the County of Maui. Had the Supreme Court decision gone the other way, in favor of the county, environmentalists feared the entire Clean Water Act, which regulated pollution discharges into waterways since 1972, would have been gutted into nonexistence—which was no doubt Trump's goal.

That the County of Maui, ostensibly dominated by the Democratic Party, could become a useful idiot to right-wing extremists hell-bent on eliminating every federal environmental protection they could find, wasn't particularly shocking to me—infuriating, absolutely. But shocking? Nope.

There's long been a feeling on Maui that the way of doing business in the continental United States doesn't necessarily work on the island, and there's truth to that. Small island living is vastly different than that afforded by a large nation interconnected by roads. But there's a nasty corollary to that attitude that is also found on island, one that often infects its public officials: the notion that rules, laws and customs of the United States don't apply to Maui. I saw this in the way Maui police officers arrested Tommy Russo, my publisher, one morning in 2012—the same year the county got sued over the sewage treatment plant. He was filming one of their operations that was causing a great deal of traffic on Haleakalā Highway. The arrest was bogus from the get-go—there is nothing illegal about filming police officers doing their jobs on a public road. But the County of Maui prosecutor's office wouldn't let the matter go. The county insisted on prosecuting my publisher on nonsensical charges that he was interfering with the officers. The case dragged on for five years, reaching all the way to the Hawai'i Supreme Court. In November 2017, that panel, far more rational than the Maui PD and prosecutor's office, heard oral arguments on Hawai'i Island, using the case as a way to teach students about the importance of a free press. Their unanimous decision, handed down the next month, dismissed the case, finding that not only had Russo complied with the orders of the arresting officers, but that the filming of police officers in the course of their work was protected by both the Hawai'i and U.S. Constitutions. Though the county prosecutor's office did announce that they wouldn't appeal the ruling, they continued to insist to the media that they'd been right to prosecute Russo.

At the same time the county's legal justice system was setting fire to public money in an effort to prosecute the publisher of *Maui Time,* it was also crafting arguments that the federal Clean Water Act didn't apply to its treatment of sewage in West Maui. The hubris was overwhelming, and it had long been clear to me that I wasn't the only one on Maui outraged at it all.

Sharyn Matin was one of those people. As far back as 2004, she and the community organization West Maui Preservation Association (WMPA, one of the plaintiffs in the 2012 case against the County of Maui, which members pronounced as "Wompa") had been tracking bacteria and pollution around the West Maui sewage facility. An attorney, West Maui resident and founder of WMPA, she had long advocated for tighter regulation of major condo and resort development in North Beach, a then-sparsely developed coastline immediately north of Kā'anapali. When I first met Matin, North Beach was essentially empty—you could park in a dirt lot (for free) and walk along a largely empty stretch of beach where trees grew right up to the sand. That's of course all gone today, replaced by a very crowded beach lined with tourists staying at the sprawling timeshares that now line the shore.

In June of 2006, Matin took me on a brief tour of the Honokowai Channel, which ran near the sewage treatment plant. During and in the days immediately following big storms, it was pretty common to see a plume of brown water fan out across the shallows from the mouth of the channel. It starts in the Honokowai Valley, way up in the West Maui Mountains, then runs to the sea, finally terminating on the northern edge of the Kaʻanapali Shores Resort on the Westside. Even on dry days, more than a few nearby locals have looked at the channel—and the big sewage treatment plant that lay just across Honoapiʻilani Highway—with suspicion and concern.

Water tests, funded by WMPA, showed excessive quantities of bacteria in the water—so much so that in 2007 Matin told the state Environmental Planning Office that she believed that high bacteria readings, coupled with "the proximity of the channel to a major sewage treatment plant," were evidence of a "public health hazard that should be addressed expeditiously."

During our visit, I quickly saw why Matin was so concerned. In the waters immediately on either side of the channel mouth, children played in the shallows. The channel itself terminated just shy of a low berm lying on the sand, but during heavy rains, water was known to flow over the sand, directly into the ocean. Just a few yards mauka of the beach, a small footbridge connected the Kaʻanapali Shores beach path with the private condos on the other side of the channel. Near the footbridge, there were even a few stone benches and a trash can for guests wanting a "riverwalk" scene to smoke, though the water in the channel was low, dark and rather murky.

A few minutes upstream, where the channel diverted into three concrete spillways that ran underneath Lower Honoapiʻilani Road, Matin and I walked across a second footbridge. The channel was pretty dark as it ran beneath the road, but from the middle of the footbridge, we could see two manhole-sized metal doors on either side of the channel that clearly led into the sewer system.

I knew the situation was bad then, but I didn't have a clue that the matter would drag on another 14 years, or that it would take a thin majority on a conservative Supreme Court to save the entire Clean Water Act from the county's unwillingness to address its own ineptitude. Standing in that channel, it was becoming very clear to me that few county officials had any interest in looking at the "big picture"—be it federal clean water regulations, the First Amendment to the U.S. Constitution or even the necessity of wildfire prevention. Instead, they would simply grab for easy answers and refuse accountability. Disasters were coming; it was just a matter of when.

Chapter 14

EDDIE AIKAU

Not everyone I covered as editor of *Maui Time* was awful. In fact, once I got to write about an authentic legend who famously refused to take the easy, safe way out. Few on Maui reached that status, but Eddie Aikau fit the bill. Go to the official webpage of the annual Quiksilver In Memory of Eddie Aikau surf contest and you'll find three curious but telling words: "WHO IS EDDIE?" Clicking on the question takes you to a page full of words and pictures dedicated to the man whose name adorns one of the biggest surf contests in the world.

Though the famous waterman and lifeguard from Oʻahu's North Shore died more than four decades ago, framing the question in the present tense works. A figure of tremendous stature and respect for most of his adult life, Aikau's influence stretches throughout Hawaiʻi to the present day. "I watched and admired Eddie Aikau out there and decided I wanted to be like him," Archie Kalepa, the County of Maui's retired chief of Ocean Safety and a big wave surfer in his own right, said in a September 6, 2012, *Lahaina News* story.

In the summer of 2013, people who'd likely never heard of Aikau got a glimpse of him through the sprawling documentary *Hawaiian: The Legend of Eddie Aikau*. It was a major production, full of all the color and adventure that punctuated Aikau's scant 31 years.

"I'm going to catch the biggest waves ever ridden and make our name famous in the surfing world," a teenage Aikau told his parents after seeing one film of the Hawaiian surfer Kealoha Kaio, according to Stuart Holmes Coleman's definitive 2001 biography, *Eddie Would Go: The Story of Eddie Aikau, Hawaiian Hero*. Audiences should always be skeptical when words like "legend" and "hero" get stuck to mortal beings, but the film makes clear that Aikau is more than deserving of such titles. Still, how do you tell a story everyone already knows? Every surfer who's ever dipped a toe in the Pacific has at least heard his name because of the immense popularity of the Quiksilver contest. And who in Hawai'i hasn't yet heard or seen the words "Eddie would go" on a shirt or bumper sticker (or "Eddie wouldn't tow" or any of the other countless variations that crop up to advance this or that cause).

For the makers of *Hawaiian* (directed by Sam George and produced by ESPN Films, Stacy Peralta and Paul Taublieb), their task was easier. Aimed at audiences who likely haven't ever ridden a wave, the film offered little new insight to anyone who grew up in Hawai'i or has at least read Coleman's book. Of course, that doesn't mean there's nothing compelling about watching Aikau talking with Jim McKay, or surfing skyscraper waves at Waimea (Without a jet ski! Or a leash!), or seeing Nainoa Thompson, who was with Aikau on that fateful 1978 *Hōkūle'a* voyage, cry when recalling what it was like to watch him paddle away from their capsized canoe. *Hawaiian* is packed with colorful film footage of life in postwar Hawai'i, but it's gripping largely because the story of Aikau is so extraordinary.

Possibly because the things he did on O'ahu were so big, it's easy to forget that Edward Ryan Makua Hanai Aikau was born on Maui in 1946. His father, Solomon, worked at Kahului Harbor as a stevedore, and young Eddie spent his first dozen years in nearby Rawfish Camp (it's all condominiums now). He went to St. Anthony's High School in Wailuku, along with his four siblings. From the accounts I've read, his youth was happy, if uneventful. A great deal of it, as remains true with most kids in Hawai'i, was spent in the water.

"Eddie spent as much time as he could in the ocean, swimming, diving and exploring the silent world below the surface," Coleman wrote. "Occasionally, Eddie would see sharks ominously cruising in the distance, but he was taught not to be afraid of them or any other creatures in the sea. The water's warm, sensual embrace was as soft and comforting as a woman's touch, and it was the beginning of Eddie's lifelong love affair with the ocean."

More than a surfer, Aikau was the definition of a waterman—he surfed, paddled, swam, dove, snorkeled and, ultimately, sailed. From his idol, the legendary surfer and Olympic swimmer Duke Kahanamoku, he adopted a relaxed, almost regal approach to surfing. His years in the water brought an understanding of the ocean that made him comfortable around the same ocean currents and sea creatures that terrify so many.

But from nearly the moment he arrived on O'ahu in 1958, death took on an ever-increasing role in Eddie Aikau's life. His father Solomon had brought everyone to O'ahu seeking more opportunities, and he certainly found one by moving the family into a Chinese graveyard in Pauoa Valley. There, Solomon and his kids would tend to the tombstones in exchange for rent-free living. Though Eddie would eventually get married and move out, his family would stay in the graveyard for many years after his death.

Riding waves at Waimea, known across the globe for its massive winter swell, brought the possibility of violent death at any moment. What's more, when he wasn't paddling out to ride, he was usually on the shore as a lifeguard—the bay's first, hired despite his never finishing high school. How many people Aikau saved at Waimea will probably never be known. The film *Hawaiian* says 500, but that's just an estimate. According to Coleman, Aikau's modesty and his strong dislike of paperwork meant he only documented a small fraction of his rescues.

Though it's often said that no one died in Waimea when Aikau was on duty, the harsh results from taking one too many risks were ever-present in his life. His brother Gerald had spent two years in the Vietnam War only to die not long after returning to Hawai'i in a late-night car accident (Aikau would occasionally hop the fence at Punchbowl and sleep at his brother's grave). A couple years later, Aikau's close friend Jose Angel vanished after attempting to dive in waters more than 300 feet deep off the coast of Maui in a hunt for valuable black coral.

All that was before he joined the crew of the *Hōkūle'a*.

"I think most of us wish if we had a chance to die a certain way, it would be doing something great like he was doing," surfer Kelly Slater says in Coleman's book. "Obviously, it was a sad way to see him go but almost a fitting end to the way he lived his life. Being lost in the ocean is tragic, but it's also romantic at the same time."

Politics wasn't Aikau's thing, but Coleman wrote that his favorite song was Country Comfort's "Waimanalo Blues," first recorded in 1975, which points to someone not at all happy with the development of Hawai'i and the long history of disenfranchised Hawaiians. The new Polynesian Voyaging Society was the perfect place for Aikau to fuse his waterman skills with his growing awareness of Hawaiian history and traditions.

Aikau was just 31 in 1978 when the Hawaiian voyaging canoe *Hōkūle'a* overturned in rough seas on its second voyage. Meant to travel from O'ahu to Tahiti and show the world that Polynesians traveled to Hawai'i by way of sophisticated celestial navigation and not dumb luck, it had beautifully demonstrated exactly that two years earlier.

But its second voyage ended just off Moloka'i when it capsized in bad weather shortly after leaving O'ahu. Wet and shivering on the overturned hull with their radio gone, the crew's hopes faded fast. There was nothing shocking or unusual about Aikau's request to paddle 20 miles to Lānaʻi to get help. Lacking options, Captain Dave Lyman agreed.

In the early 1800s, as both *Hawaiian* and *Eddie Would Go* make clear, Aikau's ancestor Hewahewa was a kahuna who guarded Waimea—a role Eddie took upon himself, and apparently took seriously. His relationship with the ocean, expansive ʻohana and huge circle of friends all pointed to a man dedicated to keeping those around him healthy and happy. Even his own name advertised his destiny—Makua Hanai roughly translates as "nurturing caregiver."

There are layers of irony surrounding Aikau's death. He set out to rescue the crew, but in the end the Coast Guard found the crew without him (though Marion Lyman-Mersereau, a crewmember who went on to write *Eddie Wen Go,* a children's book about Aikau, says that his paddling out to get help inspired her and the others to maintain hope). Aikau spent his adult life saving people who ventured out into the dangerous Waimea waters, but today he's largely remembered for paddling out himself into those same waves.

Eddie would go.

Part dare for those of us who hesitate, part honor for the man who did not, the famous phrase came from big wave surfer Mark Foo in 1986, during the run-up to the first Quiksilver Eddie Aikau contest. With 40-foot waves pounding Waimea Bay, organizers wondered what they should do. "Eddie would go," Foo told a cameraman, and the rest is history. Eddie's brother Clyde took top honors that day. As for Foo, he took his own advice once too often, and drowned in 1994 while trying to ride a massive set at Mavericks in California.

Had he lived, Aikau would be in his mid-70s now. Look at his brother Clyde in the film *Hawaiian,* and you'll see how the eternally boyish Eddie might look had he survived. Then again, had Aikau lived, it's unlikely there would be a movie called *Hawaiian.* Legends exist, but few among us ever do what's necessary to become one.

Chapter 15

ALOHA

I'm standing in the middle of the Barnes & Noble in Lahaina. It was 2015 or so. It's closed now, but at the time, it was the only bookstore selling new books on Maui. And an old white guy is mansplaining to me about how to say the word "aloha."

"It comes from the heart," he said, placing his hands over his chest. "Alo-o-oha. Alo-o-oha."

I smiled and nodded because I was there to sell copies of my latest novel, which I was still hoping he might buy, but inside I was screaming that everything he was saying was bullshit. I'd heard it all before, too—saying "aloha" that way was how the emcee at luaus always told the crowd to say it, and those few times I'd visited a luau I stubbornly refused to play along. It wasn't just wrong, it was insulting.

In his 2012 book *Aloha: Traditions of Love and Affection,* the author and researcher Malcolm Nāea Chun recounted a time in 1910 when Queen Liliʻuokalani was returning to Hawaiʻi (in fact, she was with Curtis Iaukea, Sydney Iaukea's great-great-grandfather) and found herself in front of an adoring crowd. They cheered her with a hearty "alo-o-oha," exactly as you'd hear at a Hawaiʻi luau today. But the queen wasn't having it.

"Never . . . never say alo-o-oha," the queen scolded the crowd. "It is a haole word. Aloha is ours, as is its meaning."

According to Chun, pre-contact Hawaiians saw aloha as something intimate and thoughtful, not a blindly welcoming substitute for "hello" and "goodbye." In Hawaiian romantic mythologies, the word is used to show affection and deep emotion. "[A]loha is special because it upholds, reaffirms, and binds relationships," Chun wrote. "Aloha should not be taken lightly. It should not be used casually or frivolously."

This changed after the arrival of westerners, and especially American missionaries, who, as Chun noted, were "prodigious writers." By the 1860s, the depth of the word was gone, and it had taken on a variety of meanings, especially that of a salutation. The missionaries, prominent citizens now in Hawai'i, "needed to replace their own salutations and friendly, or at least customary, hello with something from the indigenous language," Chun wrote. "Aloha appeared to be what they heard." While the Reverend Lorrin Andrews' 1865 dictionary of Hawaiian words did note that "Aloha, as a word of salutation, is modern," later usage would all but eliminate this understanding.

But when Hawai'i became a state in 1959, the Rev. Abraham Akaka attempted to bring the old Hawaiian concept of aloha into the Christian church itself. The spirit of aloha, Akaka said, was the spirit of God:

> Aloha consists of this new attitude of heart, above negativism, above legalism. It is the unconditional desire to promote the true good of other people in a friendly spirit, out of a sense of kinship. Aloha seeks to do good, with no conditions attached. We do not do good only to those who do good to us. One of the sweetest things about the love of God, about Aloha, is that it welcomes the stranger and seeks his good. A person who has the spirit of Aloha loves even when the love is not returned. And such is the love of God.

It is very difficult to reconcile those words with the ubiquitous use of "aloha" today for reasons of marketing and public relations. And the commodification of aloha happens everywhere today. Hawaiian Airlines has their "Sharing Aloha Series" of short videos in which company employees talk about family recipes or how to make a lei or speak basic Hawaiian words. Hawaiian Tropic sunscreen asks you to "say aloha to the sun!" Aloha Waste, a trash company on O'ahu, says it believes "in preserving the future of our beautiful state." Roberts Hawaii, which operates tour buses, says Queen Lili'uokalani defined aloha as meaning "to learn what is not said, to see what cannot be seen and to know the unknowable," and then tells tourists, "Don't be afraid to greet your hotel attendant or grocer at the store with a simple 'Aloha' while holding its true meaning close to your heart."

Then there are "aloha shirts," what the rest of the world calls "Hawaiian shirts." Usually colorful to the point of being ostentatious, they symbolize a laid-back party attitude. They can range from being cheaply manufactured to extremely expensive and well made. Muted, almost pastel versions are preferred by bankers and real estate brokers, and are sold in ABC Stores and Costco; those desiring more luxurious versions can try Tori Richard and Tommy Bahama. That the violent, right-wing extremist Boogaloo movement has also adopted aloha shirts is both humorous and disgusting.

Then there's the idea known as the "aloha spirit." Few, if any Hawaiians, speak of this. It's an invention that came after contact, and is often used as a bludgeon to keep locals in line.

On February 16, 2014, a video appeared on YouTube showing a young local man repeatedly cursing some white people at Kalama Beach Park in Kīhei, all while they recorded him with their phone. It all started when one of the people spoke up after seeing a local guy—apparently not the guy in the video—throw something at a nearby dog. "This is Hawai'i, we do whatever we fucking want out here, abuse dogs, hit women, that's all we do," the guy on the video says. He then curses them, and white people in general, for one minute and 37 seconds, every now and then throwing in a (true) line about how white people stole Hawai'i from those who were here first. It's appalling, ridiculous, ghastly and even a little funny, and for all those reasons instantly went viral after a local Facebook news group called MauiWatch posted it online. Over the next two years, it brought in a little more than 420,000 views—a respectable number, sure, but it was no Gangnam Style, which at the time was bringing in tens of millions of views.

Like most residents, I got a kick out of the Kalama Park video, then forgot about it. Every place has troublemakers, and one of Maui's happened to get recorded saying things that ran counter to the "aloha spirit" that most people around the world associate with Hawai'i. But I was reminded of the video during a chat in September of 2015 with two county officials who wanted to teach aloha to residents. They were talking about a new Maui County Office of the Hospitality Industry Advocate (OHIA) they were trying to set up. Though nearly two years had passed, that video was very much still on their minds.

"That Kalama Park video—that's not who we are," said David Ching, who at the time was the county's First Assistant to the Managing Director and was to be in charge of the new office. "Maybe we need to be reminded of it."

Working with fellow county official Ipo Mossman, OHIA was more of a "project" than an office, Ching said. "We only use 'office' because it fits 'OHIA,'" Ching told me.

The whole thing owed itself to the fact that the hospitality industry was Maui County's single largest economic driver. "We're the most dependent county on hospitality in the state," Ching said. "Nearly one in every two jobs is dependent on the industry. It's scary if you consider what happens if the industry goes south. It would impact massive numbers of people in the county."

This was less than five years before the COVID-19 pandemic decimated the tourist industry in Hawai'i, and yeah, the results were every bit as awful as Ching said. But what Ching was offering—something like "tourism management," which is done today—wouldn't have helped during the pandemic. In fact, the OHIA didn't seem to be anything other than another layer of county bureaucracy. The county already gave a few million tax dollars to the Maui Visitors Bureau (MVB), but Ching said that OHIA would provide the county with information and assistance it doesn't currently get from the MVB.

"We took a look at what government is doing right now to support the hospitality industry," Ching said. "We support the MVB, but what are we doing? How is it working? What we're paying them to do is market Maui County. But we don't really have a central coordinating agency for this industry. Before things get out of hand and we turn into another Waikīkī, we have to find out what's going on with the needs of the community and the needs of the industry. Are they healthy or are they clashing? It's really important for the county to balance it out before it becomes a problem."

The "fear" that Maui County would become like Waikīkī was something I heard often during my years there. Waikīkī, once wetlands along O'ahu's leeward coast, had been developed into a resort during the first years of the twentieth century. For Maui residents, it provided a fun weekend vacation spot, but its skyscrapers, expensive boutiques and huge hotels were more Disneyland and Beverly Hills than anything Hawaiian.

On one level, what Ching and Mossman were trying to do made sense. Around that time, it was known to county officials that various Maui hotels were telling visitors that they could kill time before their flights home by hanging out at Kanahā Beach Park—an area heavily used by kite and wind surfers (who don't always get along) that also has a considerable homeless population living in the brush. An office like OHIA could have alerted the hotels that such advice to tourists wasn't really helpful to anyone.

But Ching and Mossman wanted to go much further than merely coordinating information between hotels and county officials. They even produced a "Strategic Action Chart" outlining what they wanted to do, and showed drafts of it to various individuals in the community to solicit input and suggestions. One of those individuals, who had spent many years advocating for smarter, more resident-focused planning throughout the county, Maui Tomorrow Executive Director Albert Perez, was pleased to be invited, but less than impressed.

"They want more international flights, improved infrastructure for visitors and they want to teach people on Maui to have more aloha," Perez said, before calling the whole thing "pretty appalling."

While the plan was to study how tourism was impacting Maui County's roads and infrastructure (spoiler: it was a lot), and even attempt to "balance" a "world-class visitor experience" with "the non-financial needs of our community"—that last part was added at Perez's insistence—it was still abundantly clear that county officials still saw Maui's economy as first and foremost catering to tourists. And they wanted a lot more, especially from Asia. "At least 67,500" more visitors from China, Japan, Korea and Australia by 2017, to be exact.

"We may have to put up signs in a foreign language," county spokesman Rod Antone said. "Waikīkī is very Japanese-friendly. Is that something we need to look at?"

The reason for wanting more tourists from Asia is simple: most of Maui County's visitors still came from Canada and the continental United States. Any hiccup in air travel from those two areas and the county would be in big trouble. Still, I wondered how Ching arrived at such a specific number for the visitor increase. "That represents one flight per day," he said. "We did a small study, and that would have $70–100 million impact to the community in terms of revenue."

That was all the visitor growth the county wanted, because the county's roads and emergency services apparently couldn't handle anything more. "Our infrastructure is very limited," Mossman said. "If we have one flight, that's what we can handle. The fear that we'll be inundated with all these flights—we don't have the infrastructure for that. We'd be lucky to take one flight a day. The infrastructure really can't take much more."

In the late 1980s, the state tried to lengthen the runways at Kahului Airport so it could accommodate international flights. Residential opposition killed the plan (keeping Maui from becoming like Honolulu has been an effective rallying cry for many years), but by 2015 the airport was accepting direct international flights with its existing concrete.

"We already have international flights to Kahului Airport from Canada," said Ching. "They use pre-clearance airports." Those airports, which largely exist in Canada, include their own U.S. Customs offices. That means travelers go through customs before they board, allowing them to enter Kahului Airport like any passenger coming from the continental United States. According to Ching, Narita Airport in Japan may soon take on pre-clearance status.

"That market is coming," he said. "We want to be prepared."

For Perez, opening up Kahului Airport to more international flights was asking for trouble, especially in terms of invasive species, which pose considerable risks to Maui's unique and sensitive environment. "Little fire ants have gotten out of control," he told me. "They've already devastated large parts of Tahiti—people have abandoned some of their ancestral lands. No one seems to be thinking of the economic impact from invasive species. Brown tree snakes can come here in a plane's wheel well. If brown tree snakes get here, it will cost us tens of millions of dollars annually. The Maui Invasive Species Committee [MISC] does one interception of little fire ants per week. Who knows what they're not intercepting? The little fire ants even go onto the beach, the sand. They're tiny, but their bite leaves a welt that could last a week."

Ching disputed that, saying that invasive species were already a concern and additional international flights wouldn't change much. "We do have invasive species inspection areas," he said. "There are risks with flights from anywhere. Other than what we're doing right now, I don't really have an answer." Of course, the day after I spoke to Ching, *The Maui News* reported that the island's invasive species inspectors were "short-staffed"—down to about eight from a high of 17 in 2009, with four or five positions vacant "for several years."

But the last part of the OHIA plan was the most complex—and potentially the most controversial. It's what Ching and I were talking about when he brought up the 2014 Kalama Park video.

The goal was to "Improve perception of Aloha Spirit by implementing and supporting customer service improvements using the Hawaiian Culture and improve the on island (on County) visitor experience," according to the OHIA strategic action chart.

This was, straight up, teaching the island to be nicer to tourists.

"We need to get some education out there," Ching said. "A new understanding of the host culture, what Aloha Spirit is all about. Hawaiians gave the world celestial navigation and the Aloha Spirit. Aloha is a positive thing—ask anyone in the world."

According to Ching and Mossman, OHIA would start with the county government itself. "Say the county decides that all its employees should know about Hoʻoponopono [an ancient Hawaiian problem-solving process involving forgiveness] and act that way. We would then educate everyone. We're hoping that education would tell people how to act towards each other, to the community. The county has 2,500 employees—if they can go home and impress it on their families, that's a start."

Mossman added that officials in Kauaʻi County and Hawaiʻi County were already doing similar training programs for their employees.

"We'd probably do a whole series on the Aloha Spirit," said Ching. "Ipo and I are both part Hawaiian, and this is an issue for the entire community. We gotta live it, and it's kind of defeating when we think about where it's at now."

Ching and Mossman have their hearts in the right place, but this call for more aloha spirit reminded me of Sydney Iaukea's time spent working as a server at the Sheraton Resort in Kāʻanapali, and the "How to be Aloha" classes she and everyone else there had to take.

"I was deeply disturbed by these experiences, but not able to adequately formalize or articulate the problem," she wrote. "It would be many years before I could put into words the discomfort I felt for being treated like a servant, and told to do so with a smile on my face and aloha in my heart. I have been critical of the tourism industry ever since."

Which brings us back to the 2014 video of the local guy in Kalama Park. Yes, the video showed an angry guy spouting racism. But it also showed true societal troubles. Maui is very much a bifurcated island—wealthy (or at least well-off) tourists fly to the island while people born there serve them mac salad and kālua pork and clean their hotel toilets. All the old promises of weaning Maui away from tourism and bringing higher-paying tech jobs and careers have, over the last five decades, produced negligible results.

As the COVID-19 pandemic and later wildfires made abundantly clear, Maui County still makes its living catering to tourists. Given the relatively low wages these jobs carry, combined with the way in which a white-led coup toppled the Hawaiian Kingdom and then integrated the new "Republic of Hawaiʻi" into the United States, the anger exhibited by that young man in Kalama Park becomes understandable (though his actions are by no means excusable). It's funny—his full-throated ranting and raging seem almost like a cry for race war, but in the end his actions merely spurred the creation of just another layer of county bureaucracy.

"We're having three families to a house; sewage overflowing from injection wells is destroying our reefs," Perez told me. "So many things would be improved if we focused on the quality of life of our residents. Then we wouldn't have to teach residents about aloha."

County officials never implemented OHIA, though they did eventually start funding tourism management programs, which were aimed at educating visitors, not residents. But after the August 8 Lahaina fire, Mayor Richard Bissen's administration asked the County Council to transfer the tourism management fund, which by law had to be spent on management programs, to marketing, in a bid to attract more tourists to the island.

Sydney Iaukea called the move "contrary" to the whole idea behind tourism management in the first place. "A better use of the funds would be direct community aid to the residents of Maui, while the industry itself undergoes a revision to meet the needs of the residents," she told me. "The multinational corporations that run the industry also might consider the task of advertising for themselves."

The Council tabled the bill, but that doesn't mean it won't come back in some form.

CHAPTER 16

SUGAR, PART II

January 6, 2016, started out like any other Wednesday. We were scrambling to get the paper to the press (like many alt weeklies, the new issue hit the streets every Thursday), but then everything stopped. Alexander & Baldwin (A&B), the largest and most powerful landowner on Maui, announced that it would shut down the company's Hawaiian Commercial & Sugar (HC&S) mill in Puʻunene by the end of the year.

The news was huge. Beyond huge, in fact. It really was the end of an era. The Puʻunene Mill was the last big sugar operation in the state, and both its supporters and detractors were vocal and organized. Cane fires often filled the skies above Central and South Maui with acrid smoke, and soon all that would be just history. As the minutes ticked by, I watched with growing fascination as my email inbox filled with statements from public officials wanting to weigh in. Reading through them, I kept seeing the word "sad."

U.S. Senator Brian Schatz said the news "deeply saddened" him. Hawaiʻi House Speaker Joe Souki called it "a sad day indeed." Governor David Ige said he received the news "with sadness." State House member Justin Woodson (who represented Central Maui, where many cane workers lived) said he was "saddened" by how the decision would affect the mill's nearly 700 employees.

HC&S had grown, harvested and processed sugar cane into molasses on Maui since 1870. The company's 36,000-acre sugar plantation was the last such operation in Hawaiʻi, but it had fallen on hard times. A few months earlier, HC&S also lost a potentially big power-sharing deal with Maui Electric Co. that would have given it about $19 million in revenue, the *Honolulu Star-Advertiser* reported a few days after the closure announcement. But in their own statement on the mill closure, A&B officials blamed it all on agribusiness losses.

"A&B's roots literally began with the planting of sugar cane on 570 acres in Makawao, Maui, 145 years ago," A&B Executive Chairman Stanley M. Kuriyama, said in his company's January 6 announcement. "Much of the state's population would not be in Hawai'i today, myself included, if our grandparents or great-grandparents had not had the opportunity to work on the sugar plantations. A&B has demonstrated incredible support for HC&S over these many years, keeping our operation running for 16 years after the last sugar company on Maui closed its doors. We have made every effort to avoid having to take this action. However, the roughly $30 million Agribusiness operating loss we expect to incur in 2015, and the forecast for continued significant losses, clearly are not sustainable, and we must now move forward with a new concept for our lands that allows us to keep them in productive agricultural use."

The news seemed to surprise many. Lieutenant Governor Shan Tsutsui found the announcement "hard to believe." ILWU President Donna Domingo told KHON 2 News that she "was shocked." But others, like anthropologist Carol MacLennan, had a very different reaction. "I wasn't surprised," MacLennan told me a few days after the announcement. "I knew it was coming. They've been hinting at it." Indeed, though *The Maui News* consistently buried the most dire revelations in their accounts, the paper did report over the previous years that A&B was moving away from sugar, perhaps soon rather than later:

August 11, 2014: A second-quarter report shows that A&B's agribusiness posted a profit of just $400,000—down from $8.3 million in the same quarter the previous year. Sugar production as a whole is down, blamed on wet weather.

November 6, 2015: "Significant" third-quarter losses for HC&S show a $9 million operating loss for the July–September quarter. Sugar production comes in at 42,500 tons, down from 67,000 tons during the same period of 2014. What's more, company officials say that they're looking at "diversifying the crop grown on its 36,000 acres" and will make an announcement on the future of the plantation "by its next earnings call," which would take place no later than early March 2016.

December 4, 2015: HC&S announces that it is conducting a grass-fed beef experiment on 29 of its acres over by old Maui High with 15 head of cattle. One A&B official tells the paper that since November, the company has been seeking an "alternative business model," and is trying out various other ag plans.

Then just two days prior to the closure announcement, *Insider Trading Report* noted that A&B stock had fallen sharply: "2.16% during the past week and dropped 7.2% in the last 4 weeks." The mill had simply become unprofitable. It's why all the other mills in Hawai'i closed, too. Wet weather hurt, but sugar crop yields have been falling in Hawai'i for decades. The question was never if the Pu'unene mill would close, but when.

As a result of the decision, most of the 675 or so people who work in the Pu'unene mill lost their jobs. Nearly five decades of mill closures in Hawai'i had repeatedly shown that the transition away from industrialized sugar production was never easy—there just isn't enough ag around to pick up the slack, leaving many workers with no other option than to try to move over to the service industry. This is, as would be true for any news of mass layoffs, undeniably sad.

But I struggled with how much we should mourn for a company that every year churned out thousands of tons of a substance doctors say is bad for us. How many tears should we shed for a plantation that for well over a century ran Central Maui like a gigantic factory, depleting the island's soil, diverting its streams (which obliterated much of the Hawaiian taro farming in East Maui) and filling its skies with smoke? Maui Mayor Alan Arakawa called A&B's announcement "the end of an era," but I wondered if it was even truly that.

Michigan Technological University anthropologist Carol MacLennan studied every one of Hawai'i's sugar mill closures, dating back to the late 1960s. Her 2014 book *Sovereign Sugar: Industry and Environment in Hawai'i* is a sweeping look at the tremendous ecological changes sugar brought to the state. Closures like this were often traumatic, she told me. "Most of the Big Five dwindled as they diversified their holdings," she said. "But A&B has this unusual power on Maui. Because A&B has such a local identity, there's an assumption of loyalty."

The last mill may have been closing, but sugar's ecological influences over Hawai'i remained, and would likely always be there.

"The resulting erasure of what remained of the Hawaiian landscape by sugar's class of businessmen has serious consequences for sustainability in the islands," MacLennan wrote. "The faith in the human power to manipulate nature and recreate new landscapes of production continues environmental change and, when not checked, degradation." This is why MacLennan told me that sugar will still exist on Maui "in ghost form." "Sugar production is ceasing, but A&B is still there," she said. "You still have a major company with say over the acreage."

One group that certainly wasn't looking at the demise of sugar harvesting on Maui in romantic terms was the Native Hawaiian Legal Corporation. Founded in 1974, the NHLC is a nonprofit public interest law firm that's spent the last decade and a half petitioning the state—on behalf of the East Maui residents who make up Nā Moku 'Aupuni o Ko'olau Hui—to restore flows in 27 Maui streams diverted by East Maui Irrigation (a subsidiary of A&B) to

Hawaiian Commercial & Sugar (another subsidiary of A&B). It's a tedious legal process, given that HC&S uses so much water that it's long been loath to give up.

In a March 2015 hearing, NHLC attorney Alan Murakami gave a pretty good reason why: They're paying the State of Hawai'i $160,000 a year for the rights to the streams, but receive 164 million gallons per day from them, according to a March 22, 2015, *Maui News* article. Murakami noted that that comes out to less than a penny per 1,000 gallons of water—a helluva deal, considering that county water rates can be in excess of 75 cents per 1,000 gallons. Historically, plantation owners like A&B have typically retained their water rights when they close mills, MacLennan told me. But it's unclear how the mill's closure will affect NHLC's fight, since A&B has said it still wants some agricultural uses on its land.

On the day of the closure announcement, Murakami told the digital news site *Honolulu Civil Beat* that A&B's decision to stop growing sugar will certainly impact the case. "The question is how much," he said. "There's clearly nothing more thirsty than sugar cane." Earthjustice attorney Isaac Moriwake agreed. In 2014, Earthjustice helped bring about a settlement agreement with HC&S and Wailuku Water Co. on behalf of Hui O Na Wai Eha and Maui Tomorrow to restore the Waihee, Waiehu, Waikapu, and Iao Streams. "Bottom line, it's a game-changer," Moriwake told me. Because sugar requires so much more water than diversified agriculture, Moriwake said that even if A&B keeps all of HC&S' 36,000 acres in ag, they'll still require far less water than they do so now. "Now that HC&S is closing, we need to reset the fundamental assumptions," he said. "If you don't have a use, then the water needs to stay in the rivers and streams right now."

At least the cane burns ended. The method of harvesting sugar by burning the cane in the fields—the subject of considerable controversy and the first ever lawsuit in Hawai'i's new Environmental Court—ended at the close of 2016. Good riddance, because sugar production was filthy. In 2014, the state Department of Health slapped a $1.3 million fine on HC&S for 400 (!) air quality and reporting violations at the mill from 2009 to 2013. HC&S is still in discussions with the DOH over the fine and violations. The plantation could also be an extremely dusty place. One fugitive dust complaint from a particularly windy day in December 2014 led to a $3,300 violation against HC&S.

Of course, the fear that Central and South Maui could become even dustier once A&B stops growing sugar is very real. "I've read accounts from the 1800s of dust clouds hundreds of feet high and sandstorms so thick a rider could not see the ears on her own horse," historian Jill Engledow said. "I live downwind, and I'd rather have occasional cane smoke."

For their part, A&B officials insisted that they will take steps to keep Central Maui from becoming even more of a dust bowl. "As the lands are harvested, they will be replanted in a cover crop, transitioned to a replacement crop, or be allowed to return to their natural state with native ground cover," A&B spokesperson Tran Chinery told me. The use of the term "native ground cover" was ironic, given how much of Maui's native ground cover vanished when the sugar plantation came in.

Still, a huge array of questions remained over the future of the HC&S plantation. Would A&B sell off some or all of that land to homebuilders? Would a "task force" recently set up by Mayor Alan Arakawa's administration help laid-off HC&S workers find new work? Would Monsanto sweep up more land? Throughout Hawai'i, former sugar lands have given way to a variety of uses—homes, resorts, mac nut fields. It's likely some or all of that will end up here, though it'll be some time before we know for certain. In 1971, according to *Sovereign Sugar,* the Kohala Sugar Co. on the Big Island announced that it would close, putting 500 people out of work. Transition there was rough and took seven years.

In its closure announcement, A&B described three "diversified agriculture" test projects they intend to implement on their 36,000 acres, dealing with energy crops, cattle and food production. "A&B is committed to looking for optimal productive agricultural uses for the HC&S lands," A&B President and CEO Christopher J. Benjamin said in his company's January 6 announcement. "Community engagement, resources stewardship, food sustainability and renewable energy are all being considered as we define the new business model for the plantation. These are leading us toward a more diversified mix of operations."

While all of that sounded great to most residents, the words also struck anthropologist MacLennan as very familiar. "It's seen as a good thing to get away from monocrop production," she told me. "People expect that these will keep wages up, but they're always experimental. Diversified agriculture has been proposed since the 1920s, '30s. There's a long history of it in my research, but it doesn't always succeed."

There was something else in the announcements I didn't pick up at the time. When the Pioneer Mill in Lahaina had closed in 1999, the old cane fields around the operation were left to go fallow. Once managed by a huge workforce, the land was soon covered in invasive grasses that browned when the weather turned hot and dry (which was often in West Maui). Before the closures, cane fires were regular and controlled, and though they were unpleasant for anyone with respiratory issues, they amounted to a kind of nuisance. But once that land management ended, the old cane fields quickly grew into tinderboxes. In 2018, a wildfire actually did flare up in West Maui, and threatened to overrun Lahaina. At the time, county officials said a combination of quick action by first responders, both in battling the blaze and evacuating residents, and luck helped save the town.

But after the embers cooled, officials left the old cane fields alone again, and in no time they were once again covered in dry, extremely flammable brush.

On August 8, 2023, when 60-plus mile-per-hour winds from Hurricane Dora blew across West Maui, everyone's luck ran out.

Chapter 17

MAUI VISITORS BUREAU

A little more than three million people visited Maui in 2019. While that number fell dramatically in 2020 to less than 800,000 because of the COVID-19 pandemic, it shot back up in 2021 to 2.3 million. With travel restrictions further loosened in 2022, the number of visitors that year rose to 2.9 million. With this popularity, it was quite possible that 2023 would see even more tourists than the last pre-pandemic year.

But such growth came with considerable pushback from residents. Traffic on the few roads leading into West and South Maui was never great, but now it was worse than ever. Visitors covered local beaches, and, increasingly armed with ever more detailed guidebooks, mobile phone apps and YouTube videos, began unearthing secret island spots for snorkeling, diving and even fishing. Even worse, many tourists were staying away from luxurious, expensive resorts, choosing instead transient vacation rentals (TVRs) on VRBO and Airbnb that had kitchens. Lured by the far greater rental income that could be made from visitors instead of locals, property owners began converting their rooms, apartments and even houses into TVRs. Residential property values soared, eliminating homeownership for many people who'd grown up on the island.

All this led to unprecedented resistance from the County Council to further tourist expansion. In January 2022, in response to massive residential fears that the island (population: about 160,000) was in danger of being overwhelmed by waves of tourists, the Maui County Council overrode a veto from then-Mayor Mike Victorino (father of MLB great Shane Victorino) and instituted a two-year moratorium on new hotel construction. Nine months later, in a meeting lasting more than nine hours, angry residents pleaded with the nine-member Maui County Council to keep the moratorium in place.

"Please, please, please we already have too many tourists!" Kihei resident Tom Mellin said in written comments, according to local news website Maui Now. "Over-tourism will destroy Maui not just for residents, but also for tourists who want to go to someplace special. Do not listen to those who want to make a quick buck and who do not care about the long-term effects of too many tourists." Councilmember Mike Molina, who had spent many years on the panel, said he had "never seen so much passion" on the issue of tourism. But he and seven colleagues voted to repeal the hotel moratorium, though they did agree to keep a cap on transient vacation rentals.

Even as recently as a decade ago, that measure would have been unthinkable. But the council had changed a lot since I first moved to the island—the old boys' network that controlled the panel back in 2003 was no longer in power. There were more women on the council now, and many of them held a dim view of the old pro-development, pro-tourist status quo.

That status quo owed a lot to a woman named Terryl Vencyl. For over a quarter century, Vencyl worked as an agent for Maui's tourist industry: the first half as executive director of the Maui Hotel & Lodging Association, and the last half as executive director of the Maui Visitors Bureau (MVB). When she retired in 2016, visitor spending on Maui topped $4 billion, according to *The Maui News*. The daily paper did a big, positive story on Vencyl when she retired, though it contained a curious omission: the *News* reported that the MVB was the only such tourism lobbying group in Hawai'i that received more taxpayer funds from the county government than the state, which was true, but the *News* failed to report that this had been, and remains, controversial.

This was a huge deal to Vencyl, which I knew because each year she personally attended every County Council budget hearing. Every spring, the council meetings dragged on, hour after hour, as the members painstakingly reviewed the proposed budget for the next fiscal year, which then hovered between $550 million and $560 million. It made sense for her to be so attentive, because when I examined the MVB in 2013, the county was giving the organization $3.5 million every year.

This practice started in 1991, long before Vencyl ever joined the organization. The bureau would in turn use the money to promote Maui as a stellar, epic visitor destination through advertising, marketing and "press blitzes"—junkets in which travel writers get paid to fly out to Maui, stay in five-star resorts and then fly back home and write about all the wonderful, magical things they did and saw during their trip. It started out as a modest grant of $150,000, but eventually ballooned into the millions.

During budget time in 2013, I started hearing that Vencyl was spotted listening attentively at the council hearings. But she wouldn't have anything to do with me. When I called her to talk about the money the organization takes from the county every year, and the controversy it's weathered in recent years, Vencyl refused to talk until the hearings were over.

Back then it was very hard to criticize anything associated with the visitor industry on Maui. Newspaper headlines (like the one in *The Maui News* on May 10, 2013) often said things like "Economist says state's growth led by tourism." In that year, the visitor industry accounted for about 40 percent of Maui County jobs. Statewide, the numbers were even more astounding. "Tourism is on pace to support more than 166,000 jobs annually and contribute $37 million daily into our economy in 2012," Hawai'i Tourism Authority President Mike McCartney (who later went to work as Governor David Ige's chief of staff) said in a bulletin put out by his office. "These out-of-state dollars support kama'āina businesses, create new industries and help our counties to improve roadways and beautify parks. These monies also support Hawai'i Tourism Authority programs that celebrate, perpetuate and sustain our unique place, people and diverse cultures."

For years, Buck Joiner, a South Maui resident, had been tired of it all. Then one day he drove to the county's Kalama o Maui building in Wailuku, headed up to the eighth floor and filled out one of those little public comment cards. For three minutes at the beginning of the May 4, 2013, Maui County Council Budget Committee hearing, Joiner railed against the Maui Visitors Bureau.

"I'm here today to ask for fairness and honesty," Joiner said, calling attention not only to the organization's request for $3.5 million from the County of Maui, but also to it receiving an equal share from the State of Hawai'i. "That's not a small amount. Yet they come to you and say they want more."

Like many such organizations throughout the United States, the MVB is a private organization but is nearly completely funded by county and state money. In tough economic times, when Mayor Alan Arakawa couldn't get the council to go along with his plans for a new sports arena and the council was talking about raising property taxes to help pay off the county's $594 million in unfunded health and pension liabilities, $3.5 million was a lot of public money to lay out for something that pretty much exemplifies "corporate welfare."

But Joiner wasn't done. After saying he doesn't oppose the MVB per se, only "who pays for it," he insisted that the Maui Visitors Bureau behaves as though the tax dollars it receives are private donations. "It's basically a government organization, and we can't find out how their money is spent," he told the budget committee members. "I believe you're robbing from the poor and giving to the rich."

Just one councilmember, Don Couch, asked Joiner for clarification when his three minutes were up. After answering the question by saying the county needed to perform an audit of the MVB funds, the rest of the council moved on to other business. Well, most of the council—Mike White, a near and dear friend to the MVB (his day job was GM of the Kāʻanapali Beach Hotel, and he was also a former MVB board member) later referred back to Joiner. White, whose first act upon taking office in 2011 was to push for the MVB to get even more money from the county, said Joiner was all wrong, and there was plenty of accountability concerning the MVB grant.

For clarification, I called Teena Rasmussen, the director of the county's Office of Economic Development, which administers the MVB grant. "It's absolutely not true there's no accountability," Rasmussen said. "MVB's grant, as is true of all of our grants, is a reimbursement-only grant. Which means they spend the money, they have to give us an invoice and then we reimburse them for those invoices. So we have virtually a copy of every single invoice so we know exactly what those invoices purchased." Rasmussen added that her office met with MVB officials "a minimum of every 60 days" and that they "stay in touch with them on what their goals are."

Nonetheless, Joiner's criticism of the MVB grant merited serious attention for a few reasons. That Rasmussen's office looks over the invoices MVB submits is great, but it's also somewhat unique. That's because the MVB grant doesn't go through the usual process of being vetted by the Maui County Grants Review Committee, a seven-member body of appointees who evaluate grant applications under the Department of Housing and Human Concerns Community Partnership Grants (CPG) program. Joiner knows this well because he used to sit on that committee, which he called a sobering experience.

"We got 70-some applications," he said. "We went through them with a fine-toothed comb. It was really grueling. Some of these people were just skin and bones. The total requests were for $3 million, but we only had $1 million to give. The only thing we could guarantee was that everyone would be disappointed."

Running the MVB grant through a committee like that, which would hold regular public hearings, would add a layer of "accountability" to the MVB funds. But there's a better solution: simply cut off the funds entirely, and let the visitor industry itself fund the Maui Visitors Bureau.

There's plenty of precedent for this. In fact, according to the tax returns of the Maui Hotel & Lodging Association (which Vencyl ran before she moved to the MVB), that organization didn't take in any government funding.

Of course, it also had nowhere near $3.5 million in funding, but there was no reason why Vencyl couldn't do more to pass the hat throughout the multinational corporations that owned all the big Maui resorts that were seeing so much of that $4 billion in visitor spending.

And all this isn't even taking into account the nearly $3 million that Maui got from the Hawai'i Tourism Authority that year. When added to the county's MVB grant, it totaled more than $6 million in taxpayer grants to the MVB. Joiner mentioned this money in his criticism at the May 4 Budget Committee hearing, saying, "We can't find out how their state money is spent. That's considered top secret."

Of course, I thought that was absurd. But it turned out Joiner was right. Momi Akimseu, then a spokesperson for the Hawai'i Tourism Authority, told me the MVB was receiving $2,906,436 from them in 2013, on top of $2,790,018 they took from the HTA last year. Akimeseu also said the HTA gave $248,782 to visitor efforts on Moloka'i and $144,000 to efforts on Lāna'i (those grant numbers were the same in 2011). As far as what the money went for, the HTA only published a vague list back in January of "community and cultural events" the organization has supported: Whale Day, the Maui Marathon, Lahaina Plantation Days, Wailuku First Friday, stuff like that. But exactly what that support entailed was, indeed, a secret.

Chapter 18

ALBERT PEREZ

Like Vencyl, Albert Perez is a tireless advocate, though for a very different group of people. I first met him in 2015, where he was sitting at his desk in his sparse Wailuku office, which was literally around the corner from my office. He's tall, with a gentle but deliberate way of speaking. He chooses his words carefully. He's both newcomer and a veteran of the nonprofit organization Maui Tomorrow, which advocates for both increased citizen involvement in Maui life and greater prioritization of local government on the needs of residents over tourists. Perez helped found the organization in 1989, and stayed with it for its first three years, then moved to Washington state, where he worked for the better part of two decades with the state's Department of Transportation. In 2017, when the Maui Tomorrow executive director retired, Perez moved back to Maui and assumed the job.

Even nearly a decade ago, the threat of overdevelopment and excessive tourism weighed heavily on Perez. He was still optimistic, but cautiously so.

"Maui still has a chance to maintain its environment," he told me. "The place where I grew up? O'ahu? Well, they're trying. People on Maui say they don't want to be like O'ahu. But if you go to Moloka'i, the people say they don't want to be like Maui. In 1989, Dick Mayer said, 'Tourism was a medicine. Today it is a drug.'"

When Perez first helped start Maui Tomorrow, the island had roughly half the population it did when he returned. "In 1990, O'ahu had a resident–tourist ratio of 9:1, while Maui had 3:1," he said. "I can remember going to Wai'ānapanapa [in Hana] and being the only person on the black sand beach. There were 150 people there the last time I went, which was three weeks ago."

Perez grew up on Oʻahu. His parents were both teachers, and his family lived all over the island: Pearl City, Wahiawā, Sunset Beach, Makaha, Mililani. They even lived in Waikīkī for a time, in a little bungalow that's a parking lot now.

When he was in grad school, Perez did a noise study at Haleakalā. At the time, helicopters were flying 10 feet off the trails, so he took some noise meters up there. These days, anyone wanting to watch the sunrise at the summit has to get a reservation and then stand up there in a crowd of hundreds of people. But in those days, Perez was able to just drive up to the summit and watch the sunrise with no one else around. As such, his first experience at Haleakalā was just stillness, listening to nothing other than the wind blowing across the trail. In his study, Perez found that most people said the most important thing about the crater was silence. The only people who said "helicopters" were two people who'd been rescued by a helicopter.

Perez told me his main goals at Maui Tomorrow were to increase citizen involvement in local government and preserve what he called the island's rural lifestyle. "There are so many benefits to it: not being stressed out by traffic, getting home to visit with your kids, beautiful vistas," he said. "Maui is showing off every day. You know, people on Oʻahu hardly use Hawaiian words anymore, or speak pidgin. It could be a generational thing, but it's very disconcerting."

Maui Tomorrow represented a citizen-driven chance to slow Maui's overdevelopment, if not turn back the clock. Whereas developer Kent Smith had aggressively pushed a "growth is inevitable" mantra, Perez took the opposing view—that growth had to be managed, steadily and intelligently, on an island with limited resources and an economy that lacked good paying jobs outside of the service sector.

But the organization was not rigidly anti-development. If anything, it was pro-community plan. Each island in the county had one, and they were (at least on paper) supposed to be legal documents that guided development over the next generation. Unlike zoning ordinances, community plans were drawn up by citizens and then adopted by the County Council. Organizations like Maui Tomorrow wanted land developers and planning officials to treat them with respect, which didn't always happen.

When developers proposed "Waikapu Country Town," which required a land use designation change from agriculture to urban, Maui Tomorrow said it was fine. "We supported it," Perez said, and even testified before the Land Use Commission in favor of it. "The developers respected the will of the community. It's how I'd like to see developers act in the future."

The opposite occurred in South Maui, when developers proposed a Mega Mall in Kīhei on land mauka of Piʻilani Highway—the main thoroughfare through Kīhei—that had been designated as light industrial. Residential opposition was intense, but after the developers lost the first permitting round, they came back and tried to make a small portion of the project light industrial. Perez and Maui Tomorrow, guided by the community plan, which specifically stated that retail only goes makai of Piʻilani Highway in South Maui, wasn't having it. "We opposed it because we want to adhere to the will of the community," Perez told me.

There was a lot competing for Perez's attention when he took over, but one thing that loomed large was the possible development of Mākena, in South Maui. Though there was a resort down there, a few miles south of Wailea, the area was still largely untouched, with thick forests and trails through black lava fields. Back in the old days of Perez's first stint on Maui Tomorrow, the road to Mākena was littered with mufflers. Perez was down there at the beach one day, eating a taco, when he told his wife about the muffler troubles. "She thought a moment, then walked to the side of the road—sure enough, there was a rusted-out muffler," he recalled. Broken down cars notwithstanding, the water in Mākena then and now was spectacular, and Big Beach often drew big crowds of locals and tourists alike (likewise, nearby Little Beach was secluded and very popular with nudists). But the threat of condo and resort expansion had loomed over the area for decades.

In 2017, a conglomerate of developers (known in Hawaiʻi as a hui) called Makena ATC Holdings was pushing a substantial "158-unit mixed use community" for Mākena. It called for 88 multi-family units (including four "affordable" rental units), 20 single-family cottages, 26 single-family custom lots, 10 transient vacation rental units, 14 condominium units, approximately 27,300 sq. ft. of commercial space and various other infrastructure improvements. The Maui Planning Commission didn't have much of a problem with it, but three community organizations, including Maui Tomorrow, filed suit against it.

In July of that year, the suit settled. The project was still going forward, but with considerable changes. "Our negotiations will result in at least 60 units of housing, affordable in perpetuity and priced at or below median income levels, being built on Mākena resort land," Sierra Club Maui Coordinator Adriane Raff Corwin said at the time. "We have asked that first priority for these homes be given to families with historical ties to the Mākena area, giving kamaʻāina a chance to return to the land." The inclusion of affordable housing in the Mākena property itself was a huge victory (developers were too often allowed to build lower-income units far from the project itself), but the settlement agreement also reduced density throughout the entire Mākena resort lands as well as parcels closer to the shoreline, preserved on-street public beach parking around Mākena Landing, protected cultural sites and historic trails, established an independent cultural manager, and established and funded in perpetuity a community benefit fund.

"Our history of fighting for this special place goes back almost 40 years," Perez said. "The first success of this effort was the creation of Mākena State Park at Oneloa [Big Beach]. Now the future of Mākena, which has been unclear for decades, has a measure of certainty. As a community, we will need to remain vigilant, but this is a start."

Four months later, the county's Office of Economic Development released a new "Tourism Industry Strategic Plan" that called for both the preservation of environmental and cultural resources and the expansion of Kahului Airport to bring in more international flights. Though the report was supposedly crafted with the input of all local stakeholders, including Maui Tomorrow, Perez said he was caught off guard by its release. He thought the report's call for more protection of coral reefs was outstanding; the part about the airport, not so much. In fact, increased tourism could overwhelm the island's roads, water supply and waste management infrastructure, regardless of additional marine protections. "We don't have the infrastructure for the visitors we have right now," he said. "Our infrastructure hasn't changed since 1990, when they first called for direct international flights."

This was the nature of his job—win some protections for residents and take a step or two forward, then get surprised by a new threat and retreat a bit. The work was important, but it could be back-breaking, if you let it. Near the end of my time on Maui, I asked Perez what he'd learned on the job. "I realized that it's not possible to do everything myself, or even as Maui Tomorrow," he said.

Chapter 19

WAILEA

Though the problems associated with so much tourism infrastructure were apparent to me, and something I thought and wrote about all the time, the lure was also inescapable. It was a rare weekend that didn't involve Angie and me enjoying cocktails at a resort lounge in Wailea. When the skies were clear, which was most days, we'd walk the Wailea beach path at sunset, and occasionally stop and watch the show at the Te Au Moana luau for a bit. One of the best snorkeling spots on the island is in South Maui, and the last time I was there I encountered three manta rays who swam a few yards by me as though I were just another creature in the sea. The lush but meticulously manicured resorts of Wailea were minutes from our Kīhei apartment, and we would have been fools not to take advantage of them while we lived on Maui. But we would never be more than visitors to Wailea. Though there are plenty of condos there, living in that neighborhood (such as it was) was never an option for us. While we were there, new condos in Wailea were retailing between $700,000 and $1.8 million, which are low prices today. As for home sales, each year brings new records.

It wasn't supposed to be like this. Wailea, though little more than a playground for rich tourists and off-island owners, was supposed to be much more. In fact, in the late 1960s, Wailea's first developers sold the community to Maui as a revolutionary prototype community far closer to Disney's EPCOT Center than anything that exists on the island today.

Of course, Maui was a very different place back then. The rising power and influence of labor unions on Maui throughout the 1940s and 1950s had an unexpected problem—though workers on plantations were able to get raises and better benefits, the big landowners instituted hiring freezes to cut their costs. For anyone graduating from the island high schools in the late 1950s and 1960s, finding work on Maui became all but impossible.

For that reason, according to former Maui Planning Commissioner Dick Mayer, today's environmental issues and concerns weren't mentioned back then. Instead, people wanted jobs—lots and lots of jobs—so that Maui families didn't have to watch as their kids moved to the continental United States to find careers. "Decision-makers didn't consider the environment an issue back then," Mayer told me. "The agenda was, 'just create jobs to keep our kids here.'"

Two key events took place in 1959 that provided a solution: Hawai'i statehood and the introduction of jet airline flights between Hawai'i and the continental United States. Suddenly, Hawai'i was an easy, safe travel destination for millions of Americans. It was still exotic, but as a full part of the United States, it seemed far more accessible.

Hawai'i—and Maui—would need more places for the visitors to stay. The development of Kā'anapali in the early 1960s had been a major success, but Wailea had the potential of being even bigger.

In 1957, Matson—owner of the famed White Ships that had been bringing tourists to Hawai'i since the 1930s—had purchased the 1,500-acre Wailea region from 'Ulupalakua Ranch. When Alexander & Baldwin bought Matson in the late 1960s, they hired the firm Grosvenor International to develop the property to cater to exactly those tourists. The plan devised by Grosvenor, billed as "The City of Flowers" and detailed in *Maui News* stories from 1968 to 1971, makes for fascinating reading today.

The project had two main components. "It will be an entirely new town catering primarily to the tourist who wants to escape from the noise and bustle of city traffic," *The Maui News* reported in a March 15, 1969, story. "Wailea will have a permanent population of 50,000, which directly or indirectly will derive its living from the development."

Let's unpack this carefully. According to the 1970 census, Maui's population as a whole was around 47,000. But Grosvenor was planning to build a town—not a mere "community"—of 50,000 in Wailea. Though Wailea would be oriented towards tourists—complete with 11,000 hotel units—the people who worked in the hotels would also live within the Wailea town, in 8,000 apartment and residential units.

These are staggering numbers, especially considering that Wailea's population today hovers around 6,000. What's more, Grosvenor wanted Wailea to be automobile-free. "Cars will be confined to the fringes of the Community,"

The Maui News reported. "The only vehicles permitted within the built-up areas will be those providing an internal transportation system, such as tractor trains, and a restricted number of service vehicles. Special heavily screened parking areas will be provided at convenient locations."

Tractor trains moving workers and tourists alike through Wailea. But Grosvenor didn't stop there. The company also envisioned "pedestrian streets," which would "meander throughout the complex, creating a theme of discovery and surprise," according to *The Maui News*.

Grosvenor took the "city" in "City of Flowers" seriously. Wailea today is the definition of sprawl, with no walking streets or central public space—the opposite of what Grosvenor first envisioned and sold to the Maui Planning Commission. "The central core area, around which the development will grow, will be both a gathering place and the communal center," according to *The Maui News*. "It will include a variety of restaurants, shops, amusement and cultural facilities. It will feature a town square, highlighted throughout by clusters of flowers, close to Wailea's central beach."

Grosvenor estimated that it would take about 20 years to build all that out—putting a completion date around 1990. If this is starting to sound like science fiction, check out this statement from Grosvenor President Gilbert Hardman, quoted in the article: "Architecture will be simple and unobtrusive, woven into the terrain and the landscaping," Hardman said in the March 15, 1969, article. Architects need not achieve their effects by constantly imposing structures ... blatant and pretentious buildings must be avoided."

For *Maui News* readers, none of this was surprising. Six months earlier, the paper had first written that Grosvenor had big plans, saying that Hardman "believes in planning a development that fits into the existing community, rather than importing a concept foreign to the local environment and forcing it into a community."

Nearly two years later, then-A&B President Allen C. Wilcox, Jr. echoed those sentiments. "Wailea not only would not harm the natural beauty of the site, but enhance it in every possible way to make it an outstanding resort and residential community," he said in a February 11, 1971, *Maui News* story.

Throughout 1970 and the first part of 1971, Grosvenor's dream started to take shape. A site blessing took place in mid-May 1970. Wilcox was there, as were Maui Mayor Elmer Cravalho, Senate President David McClung and House Speaker Tadao Beppu, *The Maui News* reported on May 23, 1970. Just offshore, U.S. Navy bombers carried out target practice on the nearby island of

Kahoʻolawe while Reverend John Kukahiko blessed the project. After attendees planted some trees with a gold-plated shovel, Maui County Councilman Richard Caldito proceeded to win a golf driving contest.

That little golf driving contest clearly reflected the developer's construction priorities. Needing a quick source of cash, they set out to build Wailea's Blue Course first. "Of necessity, construction will come in phases," an A&B representative said in the March 9, 1971, *Maui News*. "[T]he first being the golf course and clubhouse scheduled for completion this fall." After that would come the residential development—"including units for employees," the A&B representative said, adding that they still considered their Wailea project to be a "mini city."

"Wailea will not be the type of resort where you have hotel accommodations and golf but go elsewhere for fun," the A&B rep said, ironically describing Wailea exactly as it exists today. "Wailea is planned to be an integral community with attractions and conveniences enjoyed by both tourists and local people."

Here it was, nearly the spring of 1971, and A&B's concept for Wailea still included "housing for people working on the construction and service industries for the project." It was a vision that even included a "living museum" of Hawaiian antiquities. Construction of the golf course was churning up a considerable number of ancient relics—so many that the Bishop Museum suggested Wailea include a museum. "The most unusual artifact recovered from either site was the wooden handle of a shark tooth knife, surprisingly well preserved in spite of its location in an open site exposed to the elements," *The Maui News* reported on July 15, 1970. "Bishop Museum archaeologists say that to their knowledge this is the first such specimen of a shark tooth implement, from an archaeological context."

In short, the Wailea envisioned back in 1971 was a full-blown city, full of shops, restaurants, hotels, apartments and attractions, including a Hawaiian antiquities museum. The people who worked in local hotels, restaurants and attractions would also live there, and everyone would get around not by driving cars, but by walking or riding in public shuttles.

A&B—represented by former Maui supervisor/future Maui Mayor Hannibal Tavares—sold Wailea to the Maui Planning Commission, which in the early 1970s approved the project 7–1 (Dick Mayer provided the only no vote because too many units were being proposed). "I got a concession from A&B on the setback from the ocean," Mayer told me years later. "But even then, A&B

still said that one-third of the housing would be workforce housing. They used that term—'workforce housing.'"

So what happened? Why can't residents head down to Wailea now and walk around this futuristic urban wonderland?

The answer, like so much on Maui, comes down to profits. Landowners like A&B realized they could make a great deal more money simply catering to the rich, rather than by trying to build an entire community for everyone. The Wailea Ekahi, Elua and Ekolu condos began opening in the mid-1970s. Demand was high, and prices shot up. "On April 15, 1978, some 1,200 buyers bid for 148 units to be constructed in the Wailea Ekolu Village in a frenzy similar to buying at Kāʻanapali and Kapalua," Mansel Blackford noted in his 2001 book *Fragile Paradise: The Impact of Tourism on Maui, 1959–2000*.

What developer is going to ignore that? Or, as Don J. Hibbard put it in his 2006 book *Designing Paradise: The Allure of the Hawaiian Resort*, "The escalating returns on Wailea's residential sales led to a scaling back on the number of units built, as higher quality was favored over density."

So much for Wailea workers actually living in Wailea. And if that's gone, it's very easy to ditch the pedestrian-friendly streets and those tractor trains. And if cars are now welcome in Wailea, why bother putting in a bunch of "cultural attractions" like museums?

Grosvenor was long gone by the late 1970s, replaced by Belt, Collins & Associates, and the vision of a big Wailea city left with them. All that remained was the land and a desire to maximize landowner and developer profits. "The Belt, Collins & Associates master plan anticipated Wailea having a population of 9,000," Hibbard wrote. "Thanks to the positive response to the more upscale residential offerings and attendant scaling back of the resort, Wailea only had a population of a little over 5,000 in 2000."

Because where land development on Maui is concerned, upscale beats local. It's not even close, and it's only getting worse. Today Wailea is paradise for the rich, but it could have been a wonderful home for anyone, regardless of wealth.

In August 2021, more than three years after we left Maui, an investment banker sold his 21,700-square foot Wailea mansion to a retired hedge fund CEO and a Hollywood actress for $45 million, according to the Associated Press. We used to pass this mansion, located on the northern edge of Wailea on a street of similar beachfront mansions, on our way to sip a rum drink at the Andaz or the Four Seasons or Monkeypod Café or even Tommy Bahama's.

It just so happened that the agent who brokered the deal is a friend of mine. In fact, before he went into real estate, he was one of our favorite bartenders at Tommy Bahama's. He's a nice guy—a thoughtful, conscientious guy who reads the news and doesn't like to see cruelty and suffering in society. Even now, thousands of miles from Maui, I think about this often—how nice, decent people just doing their jobs perpetuate a system that doesn't allow Hawaiian people to live on Hawaiian land.

CHAPTER 20

MAUI NŌ KA ʻOI

I'm in Long Beach, sitting at my desk, arranging this book. Taking a break, I thumb through the latest copy of *Maui Nō Ka ʻOi* magazine. The publication has been around for a quarter century, and though I bought the issue I'm looking at in the fall of 2022, it looks like it hasn't changed in at least the last decade. The magazine is 90 pages of advertisements and editorial, though like many such magazines named for the cities they cover, it's often difficult to tell one from the other.

There are a dozen incredibly vibrant full-page ads to thumb through before you get to the table of contents—ads for realtors, Rolex watches, Alaska Airlines, the shipper Pasha Hawaii, and local tourist attractions like the Maui Ocean Center, Whalers Village and the Old Lahaina Luau. It's as though settler colonialism itself bankrolls the publication. A note from the publisher (a white woman) says she's retiring after 40 years in publishing, though I'm sure the ad for her real estate broker husband (which appears one page prior to her note) will still appear in future issues. A brief story from the editor highlights a particular species of the hala pepe tree that's endemic to Maui and endangered, while a much longer article (also by the editor) profiles a Haiku resident who built a museum dedicated to Maui's World War II past on his land, which during the war housed a base for the 4th Marine Division. Other major feature pieces include a photo essay on a stunning midcentury modern mansion in Kahana, just north of the Kāʻanapali resort, and a story on a local chef who recently won a major award from the magazine's own annual awards show cooking recipes for the magazine's top editors at the retiring publisher's house. Then there's the "Who's Who" section, a two-page spread of tiny photos of chefs, restaurateurs and realtors gathering at galas around the island. By the time I got to the lavish spread on the mansion in Kahana, where the writer felt the need to define "makai," one of the most common Hawaiian words used today (it means "towards the ocean"), I knew exactly who the author was writing for.

The magazine is filled with Hawaiian words (its very name translates loosely as "Maui Number One"), but most of the people writing and editing stories are white. This is not surprising to me, given that the audience of the magazine has always been rich people who weren't originally from Maui. I covered this audience a lot for *MauiTime* because they made for colorful copy, and readers deserved to know who really owned the island. Buyers from outside Hawai'i have accounted for a huge percentage of home sales on Maui for at least as long as I've been studying the island, and this hasn't changed—in April 2022, *Pacific Business News* reported that more than a third (36%) of all home sales on Maui in 2021 were to buyers from the continental United States. "And because a lot of the most expensive homes were sold to mainland and foreign buyers, local purchasers accounted for just 52% of the $3.6 billion in sales, according to an analysis of the 2021 buyer statistics report from Title Guaranty Hawaii," PBN reported. This has led to an estimated 15,000 housing units—investment properties and vacation rentals—sitting vacant in Maui County, at a time when the county needs at least 10,000 new homes for residents, *Honolulu Civil Beat* reported in April 2022. This isn't even counting the whole Department of Hawaiian Homelands fiasco, in which tens of thousands of Kanaka descendants have been living and dying across the state on a waitlist for one of the nearly 100,000 homesteads opened by Congress back in 1921. While these upside-down priorities, in which society values speculative investing over housing actual residents, exist in major cities all over the country, they do extra damage on a small island like Maui, in which the economy is driven by tourism and agriculture and very little else.

As such, I decided early on to report on what rich people were doing to Maui, though hopefully without being heavy-handed. To this day I wonder why the manager of the Montblanc store in Wailea (which has since closed) allowed me to hang out with her staff during their event for valued customers back in the spring of 2004. Maybe it was because I'd been on the island less than a year. In any case, it was fun talking with extremely wealthy (and mostly white) customers who drove from places like Kā'anapali (about an hour away) and used their Visa cards to buy $11,000 fountain pens. "We wanted to send engraved, wax-sealed invitations," the store manager had told me shortly before the event began. "But the post office suggested we not go that route. They said they would get hung up [in the sorting machine]." So the manager had her staff deliver the invitations personally.

The irony is that though so many people are paying millions to move to Maui, the houses they're buying in places like Kāhana, Kāʻanapali and Kapalua aren't particularly well made. In late 2003, a single mother with two teenage sons told me her six-year-old house in Kāhana was already falling apart—rotten porch boards, peeling paint and leaky pipes. Plumbers told her the builders had installed the wrong types of pipe. "It was supposed to be copper, but instead they installed black plastic," she said. Then in 2007, a group of owners in Kapalua's Honolua Ridge Estates complained to developers that their new, supposedly lavish neighborhood was plagued with mud-clogged drainage inlets, potentially unsafe drainage basins and poorly graded roads. They even commissioned an expensive report on the troubles that took four months to complete, but the developers didn't want to admit they'd cut so many corners.

Nobody ever said being wealthy equaled being smart, or careful.

Chapter 21

KALEIKOA KAʻEO

Kaleikoa Kaʻeo is a legit revolutionary. What happened to him in the last year of my life on Maui was one of many radicalizing events that took place around Hawaiʻi—events that laid much of the groundwork for both the organization of aid in the hours and days immediately following the August 8 Lahaina fire as well as the community outrage.

The power of language to help, and hurt, was well known to the Americans who overthrew Liliʻuokalani's kingdom. It's why they made it illegal to teach Hawaiian. It was a calculated, racist act aimed at snuffing out the culture entirely. Though speaking the language remained legal, many teachers disciplined or even hit Kanaka students who spoke Hawaiian instead of the preferred English. Incredibly, this remained the status quo until the 1970s (a time of reborn support for indigenous culture known as the "Hawaiian Renaissance"). Though Hawaiian became an official language in the State of Hawaiʻi in 1978, acceptance has been slow.

In January 2018, Kaleikoa Kaʻeo, the Hawaiian Studies professor at UH Maui College and sovereignty activist, appeared in District Court Judge Blaine Kobayashi's courtroom. The previous August, Maui police officers had arrested Kaʻeo and five others for allegedly blocking a convoy of construction equipment headed up to the new Daniel K. Inouye Solar Telescope atop the 10,000-foot dormant volcano Haleakalā. It wasn't the first arrest for him, either—in July 2015, Kaʻeo and a few other protesters had laid down in front of a convoy of trucks carrying telescope equipment as it was leaving the Mokulele Central Baseyard, according to *The Maui News*. Kaʻeo, his comrades, and many others throughout Hawaiʻi view Haleakalā (and Mauna Kea on Hawaiʻi Island) to be sacred, and oppose the construction of large telescopes there. It's not that they're anti-science—it's that they view the entire process, set in motion by a government they believe is illegitimate, as insulting. Now in court in early 2018, Judge Kobayashi called Kaʻeo's name.

Kaʻeo responded in Hawaiian, which Kobayshi ignored. Kobayashi called his name a few more times, and Kaʻeo responded to each request in Hawaiian. But Kobayshi ignored Kaʻeo each time. After a few moments of this, Kobayashi issued a bench warrant for Kaʻeo's arrest.

It's important to remember that speaking Hawaiian in court is perfectly legal and acceptable in the State of Hawaiʻi. By law, the court has to provide a translator to those who wish to testify in Hawaiian. Kobayashi's actions—full of condescension and hubris—were very recognizable to Hawaiian activists. And the fact that Kobayashi was of Japanese ancestry was irrelevant—to activists like Kaʻeo, the whole legal system itself, imposed on a land long ago stolen by whites, was itself a tool of the same white supremacists who toppled Liliʻuokalani's government more than a century ago.

Within minutes, Kaʻeo was outside the courthouse, surrounded by his friends and well-wishers. At least one person filmed Kaʻeo's remarks, then posted the video on Facebook, where it quickly went viral. Though Kaʻeo spoke English outside the courthouse, he said he felt that presenting his defense in Hawaiian was his best course.

"I say it's a tragedy but it's also important that these events happen because when it does, it does wake up the people, to really see what people think," Kaʻeo told the crowd. "The revitalization of our language took a lot of work to get back to the point where it is today. The destruction of our language was something that was purposely done to our people by those who profited off our oppression for all these years."

Undoubtedly horrified at the storm of bad publicity now engulfing the Hawaiian legal system, the Hawaiʻi Judiciary recalled Kobayashi's bench warrant just a few hours after it was issued. But the damage was done. Two days after the fiasco in Kobayashi's courtroom, hundreds of people gathered on the large lawn outside the Kalana O Maui Building in Wailuku (where the county government is based) and demonstrated their right to speak Hawaiian.

I remember standing at the massive protest at the Kalana o Maui Building and seeing Albert Perez. His height made him easy to spot in a crowd, so I walked over to him. He was fascinated by the size of the crowd, and the speed with which organizers had set it up, but the protest didn't surprise him.

The reversal of the bench warrant turned out to be just the first backstep the court system would make in correcting the heavy-handed police response to Kaʻeo's protests. In fact, in January 2022, the Hawaiʻi Supreme Court ruled that there wasn't sufficient evidence to warrant a disorderly conduct conviction stemming from Kaʻeo's 2015 arrest. And that was it, as far as any criminal case against Kaʻeo was concerned. But the damage to the perceived legitimacy of the entire system was long done. The power of Kanaka activism was also now an irrefutable force, a real player in Hawaiian politics, power and especially water rights, though longtime officials would need more than one lesson to understand that.

One arrived a few days after the August 8 Lahaina Fire, when *Civil Beat* posted an article extensively quoting West Maui Land Co. officials who strongly suggested that Kaleo Manuel, an official at the State Department of Land & Natural Resources who was also Hawaiian, had put too much emphasis on returning water (that was once diverted to West Maui Land) to Hawaiian West Maui taro farmers. As such, the land owners argued in the article, West Maui firefighters had insufficient water to fight the August 8 blaze. It was nonsense, but at the same time, the DLNR transferred Manuel, though agency officials refused to explain why. Manuel had long been popular for his emphasis on returning water that had been diverted for sugar interests to Hawaiian farmers, so I wasn't surprised that within hours of Manuel's removal, Native Hawaiian activists statewide responded with anger. They denied that a few farmers somehow used up enough water to deprive firefighters of defending Lahaina, and demanded that Manuel be reinstated. It took a couple months, but after extremely contentious hearings, the DLNR board relented and gave Manuel his job back.

Chapter 22

AGE OF STUPID

What happened to Kaʻeo and Manuel was stupid and unnecessary, two things I saw often in state and local government. There was a general sloppiness in government at all levels in Hawaiʻi. It unquestionably was still in effect in the summer of 2023 when Herman Andaya, the head of Maui County's Emergency Management office, decided to attend a conference on Oʻahu during a Red Flag warning. As a result, he was off island when Lahaina burned. That he was allowed to resign a couple weeks later for "health" reasons was both laughable and insulting.

Sometimes the stupidity was merely humorous, like the time in late 2017 when the Maui County Auditor's office released a report noting that questionable overtime policies were driving up costs at the county Fire Department at an alarming rate. Most government officials, even at the county level, would have reacted with some kind of measured response that either politely disagreed with the auditor's findings or graciously accepted the findings.

But not the Maui Fire Chief.

"I believe it is not in your right to dictate to the Fire Department that you have no experience or inclination on how to operate or manage," Chief Jeffrey Murray wrote to Auditor Lance Taguchi. "By doing so, you greatly disregard firefighters and compromise the safety of a [sic] community."

Taguchi's fiery (sorry, not sorry) and incredibly sarcastic response to Murray's barely literate criticism was pure journalistic gold.

"Regarding the Fire Chief's statement that ʻ . . . you have no experience or inclination on how to operate or manage,' we admit we do not have any experience managing a fire department," he wrote. "However, this audit is heavily based on financial analysis and financial management of resources, or 'numbers.' We KNOW numbers. And those numbers say the Fire Chief has a very big problem on his hands. Regarding the Fire Chief's statement that ' . . . you greatly disregard firefighters and compromise the safety of the community,' again, we are not firefighters and we must point out we never claimed to be. We believe one does not need to be a firefighter to recognize that the Fire Chief's statements conflict with what the MFD is actually doing. Seeing our audit results mischaracterized—particularly when the findings and recommendations are based on the MFD's current practice—makes us lose confidence in the Fire Chief."

Murray retired eight months later, after nearly three decades with the department.

Murray's tirade against the county auditor was funny to me. What wasn't funny was what happened on the morning of January 13, 2018. What happened was something extraordinarily frightening and stupid.

A few minutes after 8:00 a.m., the state's Emergency Management Agency (EMA) sent out an alert to everyone's mobile phones saying a ballistic missile was inbound to Hawai'i. For 38 minutes, that alert hung in the air like a guillotine blade—the rope had been freed, and we were all just waiting for the slice. News organizations and officials like Representative Tulsi Gabbard started posting updates that it was all a mistake five to 10 minutes after the initial alert went out, but by that point huge numbers of people—residents and tourists—were already terrified.

I was relatively fortunate during the scare, because my phone was on silent and in another room when the first alert came through. By the time I checked my phone, news had already reached Twitter stating that the alert was bogus (though I did experience a frantic 30 seconds or so while I scrolled through my feed looking for confirmation of the alert). Ironically, I had been playing the video game Fallout 4 at the time the alert came through, a game that literally begins with a family relaxing on a weekend morning when they hear that all-out nuclear war has broken out.

Others had to deal with tears and uncertainty and mind-numbing fear that will probably stay with them the rest of their lives. Even 10 minutes can be a hellish eternity if you have a child who suddenly thinks his or her entire world will turn into fire at any moment.

The actual alert was unambiguous and terrifying: "BALLISTIC MISSILE THREAT INBOUND TO HAWAII. SEEK IMMEDIATE SHELTER. THIS IS NOT A DRILL." But as I read those words, yelling at me in all-caps, I couldn't help but notice that the doomsday sirens hadn't gone off. That made no sense to me, which is why I immediately checked social media (a text from a friend sent around the same time as the alert asking me if I'd also gotten it only added to my urgency). But for many who don't use social media, their only recourse was to check the radio or television, where they either saw the alert broadcast again or regular broadcasting—neither of which was reassuring.

It took state officials an agonizing 38 minutes to send out a second phone alert saying the whole thing was an error. Federal Communications Commission (FCC) Chair Ajit Pai angrily denounced that the next day.

"The false emergency alert sent yesterday in Hawaiʻi was absolutely unacceptable," FCC Chair Ajit Pai said in a January 14 statement. "It caused a wave of panic across the state worsened by the 38-minute delay before a correction alert was issued. Moreover, false alerts undermine public confidence in the alerting system and thus reduce their effectiveness during real emergencies." Pai added, "Based on the information we have collected so far, it appears that the government of Hawaiʻi did not have reasonable safeguards or process controls in place to prevent the transmission of a false alert."

Hawaiʻi House Speaker Scott Saiki was angry, too.

"This system we have been told to rely upon failed and failed miserably today," he said in a statement released shortly after the false alert was countermanded. "I am deeply troubled by this misstep that could have had dire consequences. Measures must be taken to avoid further incidents that caused wholesale alarm and chaos today. Clearly, government agencies are not prepared and lack the capacity to deal with emergency situations. Apparently, the wrong button was pushed and it took over 30 minutes for a correction to be announced. Parents and children panicked during those 30 minutes."

And Representative Kaniela Ing, D-South Maui, was furious. "Hospital patients were moved," he tweeted not long after the alert was cancelled. "My friend's mom called her crying, saying goodbye. My other friend was huddled downstairs with her toddlers. This is not ok."

* * *

What happened in Hawaiʻi on the morning of Saturday, January 13, 2018, was a disaster. A huge portion of the state became utterly terrified that their lives were about to end in extreme violence. Their fear was real, and the actions they took during those minutes between the alert and their discovery that the whole thing was an error were often heartbreaking.

"I made the bed for some inexplicable reason, trying to act normal," one person said on social media shortly after the erroneous alert was canceled.

Another, who had just arrived on Maui, was dumbstruck. "[I] realized I had no idea where [the] shelter is," she said. "[I] Tweeted goodbye to friends and family on the mainland. The news had NOTHING while it was going on. Was going to get in bed with my boyfriend to wait for the end, like in Rogue One."

The trauma was very real. A neighbor of mine at the time, who was born in Hiroshima and was only alive because a wardrobe had randomly fallen in front of her mother during the August 1945 atomic bombing of the city, shielding her from the blast, never spoke to me about the alert. It was simply too painful.

About 18 months after the alert, two University of California, Irvine researchers used data from Twitter to determine that fear from the alert lingered for a week for many people after they learned the whole thing was a false alarm.

"Low prealert anxiety users expressed more anxiety at the onset of the alert and for longer relative to other groups," stated their study. "Moreover, anxiety remained elevated for at least 7 days postalert. Taken together, findings suggest that false alarms of inescapable and dangerous threats are anxiety-provoking and that this anxiety can persist for many people after the threat is dispelled."

Nearly two years after the alert, friends of mine told me the whole thing still bothered them. One friend who no longer lives on Maui said that it caused her anxiety for a few weeks. "I didn't have confidence in our state government after that," she said. "Also, I felt anxiety because I knew that I wouldn't have been able to reach my dad to say goodbye. Knowing that if it had been real, I would have died without being able to say goodbye. That haunted me." Another friend who still lives on Maui said that even now, talking about the false alarm unnerves her. "I feel like an event like that actually could happen if something doesn't change. Out here, we're isolated and cut off. We'd be screwed."

But as all of it was happening—as I was reading news stories and tweets and Facebook posts from Maui residents who were clearly still shaking from the alert—I kept thinking how it was madness that a mistake like this was even possible. We truly live in an Age of Stupid, and we can't take two steps before being reminded of it. The mindless Tide Pod Challenge makes for amusing reading, but is there a more perfect analogy for our times? We live in an Age of Stupid because there's no value in being intelligent.

You only had to watch a few minutes of the press conference held a few hours after the alert with Governor David Ige (who somehow won re-election later that year) and EMA Administrator Vern Miyagi (who four months prior had inexplicably agreed with a CNN reporter's suggestion that people who found themselves on a beach during an alert could hide in caves). Both men made clear that, although they were really "sorry" about the "error," they wouldn't fire anyone who was involved in it (Miyagi did tell everyone that "the guy" who made the error "feels terrible about it").

"Today is a day our community will never forget," Ige said at the press conference. "I know firsthand how today's false alarm affected all of us here in Hawai'i, and I am sorry for the pain and confusion it caused. I, too, am extremely upset about this and am doing everything I can do to immediately improve our emergency management systems, procedures and staffing." He later added that "We have already taken action to ensure this doesn't happen again," though he didn't explain what that would entail.

Miyagi then said he would "take responsibility" for the false alert. "This is my team," he said at the press conference. "We made a mistake."

Neither man inspired much confidence. Neither seemed to grasp that many people experienced truly horrifying moments (especially if they had children), and how angry we all got after news that it was all a false alarm started to spread. They didn't elaborate on how exactly they changed the procedures for sending out test alerts and real alerts, and refused to answer reporters' questions about who exactly made the error, saying it was a "personnel matter." Even more alarming, neither Ige nor Miyagi could explain why many people in Hawai'i didn't receive either the initial alert or its cancellation notice, though they said they'd look into it.

There were so few details on how the false alert was sent and how they were going to make sure it never happens again that it would have calmed many nerves if Miyagi had just grabbed the microphone and said that he ordered his deputy to put tape over the death button.

The *Honolulu Star-Advertiser* reported that the error happened in a "routine internal test during a shift change," but that doesn't really tell us anything. Follow-up reporting by *Honolulu Civil Beat* and *The Washington Post* revealed that extremely poor alert system design—not mere operator error—probably played the biggest role in the catastrophe. The employee who triggered the alert was apparently faced with a dropdown menu of options like "PACOM (CDW)—STATE ONLY" and "DRILL—PACOM (CDW)—STATE ONLY;" the employee reportedly chose the first one instead of the second one. There was also a two-step authentication requirement to send the alert, but that doesn't seem to have made any difference (two days after the false alert, Ige appointed Brigadier General Kenneth Hara to carry out a "comprehensive review" of the state's emergency management procedures).

And I haven't even gotten to the fact that Hawai'i Tourism Authority President George Szigeti also spoke at the January 13 press conference. "Hawai'i is open for business," he said, answering a question no one in the entire state had asked. Later that day he issued the following statement: "We have been in contact with our tourism stakeholders to inform them of today's false alert and reassure them that Hawaiʻi's safety and security is unaffected by today's unfortunate incident. There is no cause for travelers with trips already booked to Hawaiʻi or considering a vacation in the islands to change their plans. Hawaiʻi continues to be the safest, cleanest and most welcoming travel destination in the world, and the alarm created today by the false alert does not change that at all."

For their part, Maui County officials have been largely silent on the fiasco. Indeed, in the 24 hours immediately following the false alert, I received just one statement from a county official. It was a press release from County Communication Director Rod Antone that quoted—wait for it—Rod Antone.

"This appears to be a mistake, but that doesn't mean we can't learn from this, and we should," Antone quoted himself saying in his own press release. "Remember that if this attack had been real, people should 'get inside, stay inside and stay informed.' What this means is that if you're out shopping, stay in the store; if you're at home stay at home. Don't go driving anywhere. Turn on the radio or television and listen to the news."

I know language like this is an attempt to be helpful, but it's not optimal. The phone alert is designed to give Hawaiʻi residents 15 minutes' warning to take shelter. This is a questionable gesture, since there are few, if any, proper nuclear bomb shelters in the state. Nonetheless, state officials say that anyone who hears the alert needs to immediately "shelter in place"—a euphemism that basically means huddle inside a building, away from glass, and hope for the best (officials also recommend "sheltering in place" for 14 days).

* * *

Seriously, all this is stupid. The state's missile alert sirens (which did not go off during the alert) are stupid. The fact that an alert gives residents a mere 15 minutes to "find shelter" is stupid. The whole fear that North Korea is on the verge of nuking us is doubly stupid, especially given the fact that Hawaiʻi itself is conquered territory and that over the last two decades, the United States has been responsible for raining more fire and iron onto people around the world than anyone else. The outrageous bluster that President Donald Trump regularly spewed against North Korea, arrogantly threatening them with nuclear annihilation, was beyond stupid.

Some said they were never worried because our missile defense systems would have shot down any incoming rockets, which was nonsense. Even after decades and tens of billions of dollars, missile defense in the United States is, at best, a question mark. At worst, it's a flimsy sham that will fall apart at the first sign of trouble.

"The United States has spent hundreds of billions of dollars developing, testing, and fielding ballistic missile defense systems over the past few decades," Fred Kaplan wrote in *Slate* just a few months prior to the false alert. "But in tests, these systems hit their target only about 50 to 60 percent of the time. And even this record exaggerates how they would likely perform in an actual conflict. In the tests, everyone involved knows ahead of time when, where, and at what angle the missile will be launched. Also, with only a couple of exceptions, the tests have aimed an interceptor against just a single target—whereas, in a real war, the attacker would almost certainly fire a volley of missiles. The real attack might even happen at night, whereas all of the tests have been conducted in daytime."

Of course, this entire debate is stupid, useless and insulting, especially given the fact that—and this is the best part—North Korea did not have the capability of launching a nuclear missile at the United States. The Secretary of Defense himself said this publicly a month before the false alert.

"North Korea's November ICBM 'has not yet shown to be a capable threat against us right now,'" Secretary of Defense James Mattis said during an off-camera briefing with reporters at the Pentagon, according to CNN.

What Mattis said had been reported a lot. Wanting a nuclear-tipped intercontinental ballistic missile and testing one are not the same thing as deploying one. Sure, the North Korean regime was trying to field one as fast as they can—who wouldn't, given all the times Trump has threatened them with extinction?—but that didn't mean they had one that could reduce Hawai'i to ashes.

The January 13 alert was a mistake, but the Age of Stupid we all live in is very real and every bit as scary. The mistaken assumption of a missile launch can all too quickly end up provoking a real all-out strike. We've known this danger since the United States began building missiles, which by their very nature are not recallable. Indeed, President John Kennedy was reportedly so afraid of an accident precipitating war that he constantly referenced Barbara Tuchman's The Guns of August, which detailed the miscalculations that led to World War I, in his discussions with his military commanders. A report in *The Guardian* that the Trump Administration wanted to develop new, more "usable" nuclear weapons only added to the danger.

We're all in this mess because nothing substantial has changed since the Cold War. We say the Soviet Union is gone and we've gotten rid of many nuclear weapons, but we still hold more than enough to burn the entire world many times over. What's more, we—the richest and most powerful nation in history—still regularly bomb the poorest nations into rubble and threaten others with nuclear fire.

We do all this in large part because we've forgotten how not to do it. We long ago became what our folklore always told us we're against—a giant war machine that exists solely to protect access to the capital and raw materials we need to sustain ourselves. And so we lie to ourselves about our actions around the world, which is beyond stupid.

CHAPTER 23

THE WHITE LOTUS

That said, fictionalizing Hawai'i can still be fun. Somehow during my time as *MauiTime* editor I found the energy and time to write three novels, all set on Maui. Published by tiny Event Horizon Press—the owners and operators, Barbara and the late Joseph Cowles, had once been Maui residents—the novels followed the adventures of Charley Ridgway, a good-hearted but cynical bartender in Kā'anapali. Maui, I had discovered early on during my reporting, had the disparity of wealth, roguish police force and organized crime history that made it ripe for contemporary noir treatment. Though fiction, the novels sometimes played off real events and personalities I'd come across in my research, but couldn't report on for one reason or another. Writing them allowed me to vent in ways I couldn't as *MauiTime* editor, though they never made me much money (getting published by a small press often means doing your own marketing, something I profoundly suck at). While I did a few book signings around the island, the ever-shrinking supply of Maui bookstores made the events increasingly difficult to arrange.

The extremely popular TV program *The White Lotus* is something else entirely. Season 1 of the HBO series took place on Maui (though I'm not sure the island was ever specifically mentioned in the show). While it's a lot of fun to watch places I know featured in movies and television shows, it's not fun to sit there wondering what the show's creators (or in this case, creator: Mike White both wrote and directed *The White Lotus*) were thinking as they crafted the six-episode series. Let me be clear: I really wanted to like this show. Mike White, the show's writer and creator, had been clear in interviews that he wanted to use the show to shine a light on white privilege. "My hope is that while obviously a lot of the white privileged people are oblivious to certain things, at the same time the idea is to see it from a humanist perspective in that like you see why they're defensive and why they don't see," White told *The Hollywood Reporter* when the show debuted on HBO in July 2021. "It's not necessarily trying to humanize white rich people, but at the same time, see how you can be a hero in your mind and you still are a villain to someone else and you're stamping on someone else while you're achieving your dreams."

That *The White Lotus* won five Emmy Awards speaks to both its popularity and the quality of its production, but there's an obvious problem with the whole premise of the show: White himself is a white privileged person. And while his show clearly shows white people in a Hawai'i resort in an unflattering manner, the ultimate character arcs show a degree of sympathy and empathy for them that doesn't exist for the non-white characters. I suppose a case can be made that White is simply reflecting reality, but if so, where's the fun in watching a show about silly, selfish white people screwing over locals and then going home to their silly, selfish lives?

Born of the COVID-19 pandemic, *The White Lotus* was a way for HBO to produce a show in one location relatively quickly (and safely, given the masking and social distancing requirements of the fall of 2020, when the show was filmed). While some of the show was filmed at Olowalu, the vast majority of the season was shot at the Four Seasons in Wailea, a resort I often visited while living on Maui. While not the largest or grandest of the resorts on Maui or even in Wailea, it's one of the most luxurious. A close friend once worked housekeeping there and would regale me with tales of celebrity guests behaving very badly. Another friend, who ended up working as a paparazzo, got himself banned from the resort grounds, though he often spent his day huddled in the shade on nearby Wailea Beach—public property where resort security had no jurisdiction. Though I loved visiting the hotel, I could never afford to stay there for even one night. But I have fond memories of drinking a martini and listening to live jazz in the Lobby Lounge, or sitting at the bar at Ferraro's, watching the sunset while devouring the best Italian bread I've ever had (crusty, nearly burnt on the outside, soft and pillowy on the inside).

The six-episode season concerns three groups of white tourists staying at the resort for a week. While Jennifer Coolidge's Tanya, who is staying at the resort by herself, has some wildly funny lines and bits, the show is more of a drama. There's the high-powered executive (Connie Britton) and her hapless husband (Steve Zahn). There's the rich, entitled asshole (Jake Lacy) and his hesitant wife (Alexandra Daddario). And there's the troubled rich woman who is dealing with her mother's death (Coolidge). There are also a smattering of hotel employees trying to manage their unruly guests, including Armond, the arrogant drug addict manager (Murray Bartlett) and Belinda, the kind but exhausted African American spa manager (Natasha Rothwell).

The season peaked in Episode 4. Paula (Brittany O'Grady), a relatively minor character who is not white, is talking to her lover Kai (Kekoa Scott Kekumano), a resort employee who is also not white. They are talking about her friend Olivia (Sydney Sweeney), the daughter of the high-powered executive, and Paula's need to keep her romance with Kai a secret from her.

"Why don't you want her to know that we're hanging out?" Kai asks her.

"She's tricky," says Paula.

"Isn't she your friend?"

"Yeah, she's my friend," Paula says. "As long as she has more of everything than I do. But if I have something of my own, she wants it."

That right there, is the history of white people, be it in Hawai'i, Africa, the Middle East, Southeast Asia, whatever. It's colonialism reduced to just two sentences, and it's absolutely brilliant, but the show fell apart after that. Or rather, it fell into the same white supremacist nonsense that ultimately destroys nearly everything written about Hawai'i by white people. Because at its heart, Maui and the people who are from Maui (like Kai) aren't the point of *The White Lotus*. They're backdrop, set design and plot devices. Writing in *Vox* shortly after the show concluded, the writer Mitchell Kuga (who was born and raised in Hawai'i) called Kai "a clumsy and lazy symbol of colonialism in a moment that could have taken greater care to humanize what it means to be Native Hawaiian living in modern Hawai'i."

Other than Armond, Kai is really the only person on the show who suffers any consequences. Belinda (who is not white) is definitely let down, but at the end she's basically at the same place she started. Kai, on the other hand, is hauled off to jail like so many locals while the rich white people finish their vacation and return to their lives (ethically compromised and spiritually meaningless though they may be).

Except for Quinn (Fred Hechinger), Olivia's younger brother, whose bonding with the locals at Wailea Beach leads to him running off from his parents at Kahului Airport and somehow joining the *Hōkūle'a* voyaging canoe (the very same one that capsized in 1978 and led to the death of Eddie Aikau) is outrageous science fiction. Even giving White a pass for not understanding the singular importance *Hōkūle'a* plays in twentieth-century Hawai'i, Quinn befriending and joining a local canoe club after spending a week at the White Lotus (and apparently not ever leaving the resort) is cartoonish fantasy. Canoe clubs exist all over Maui, and include any resident (Kanaka or not) who is willing to devote early morning hours to paddling. They are long-established organizations, and some even sell food at the Maui County Fair to raise funds. But they exist on a different reality plane than any paddling activity that tourists can pay for on Wailea Beach.

Clearly, for *The White Lotus* and its creators, none of this matters. Hawaiʻi is a jumble of color, musical language, epic sunsets and historical injustice, all of which is ready and available to be mined and processed by Hollywood producers looking for a quick hit for pandemic-weary audiences who can afford to pay for streaming service. In seeking to satirize colonialism, Mike White ended up replicating it.

"By scraping at imperialism, *The White Lotus* mimes a moral center but never engages the topic beyond mere gesture," Kuga wrote in Vox. "How could it, when the locals and Kānaka Maoli are depicted in only a single dimension?"

Chapter 24

"GET A JOB"

The best film about Maui is, by far, *Get a Job*. A comedy released in 2010, *Get a Job* tells the story of Merton, a slacker who decides he needs to go to work, even though he never worked before in his life. Along the way he meets William, a stressed-out job counselor who immediately dislikes Merton, but agrees to help find him work. The result is slapstick comedy on and about Maui itself. Packed with local humor, references, characters and 35 island locations (filmmaker Brian Kohne cast the film with 300 people, including many friends who aren't actors, along with Maui residents Willie Nelson and Mick Fleetwood), the film succeeds in showing what life on Maui is actually like for people who live here. That the film's stars are famous Maui musicians from the duo Barefoot Natives (Eric Gilliom plays Merton and the late Willie K plays William) adds to the local appeal. And Kohne did nearly everything on the $200,000 production, including directing, writing, producing and even editing.

Get A Job also succeeds at something the most famous comedy about work—Mike Judge's *Office Space*—failed to do, which is stay true to its own vision. Sure, *Office Space* is funny, and had some good acting, and I still to this day laugh over that scene where the guys beat the guts out of that printer in the field, but the movie ended up rejecting its own premise. It starts with Peter (Ron Livingston) declaring that he wanted to live in a world without work and just "do nothing." That was it. No more work for him. It was, in the last days of the twentieth century, the ultimate rebellion against society. But then the movie ended with him exchanging his white-collar computer screen for a blue-collar shovel, apparently finding happiness in manual labor that had eluded him in software development.

"The cynicism of multimillionaires like Mike Judge and Jennifer Aniston telling us to find happiness with a shovel is monstrous," Curtis White wrote in his 2007 book *The Spirit of Disobedience*. "All of the trust generated early in the film through damning depictions of work go spiraling away in disgust. The only answer the film provides to its big question, 'What should we do about alienation in work?' is 'Nothing—give up; find a way to conform.'"

Get A Job says right out that work sucks, and stays true to that to the end. The acting, writing and production values don't come close to *Office Space*, but Kohne stayed true to his premise, and to this day, I'd recommend *Get A Job* over *Office Space* to anyone who wants to see a comedy about work.

"The characters and dynamics are the result of the Barefoot Natives collaboration," Kohne told me in 2012. "As for the story, I was on the mainland, wondering if I should come home. This was four years ago. The workforce on the mainland was crumbling. I applied for a lot of jobs over there, and wasn't even getting a nibble. I reasoned that it would be easier to make a feature film called *Get a Job* than it would be to actually find a job. It's probably true. I struggle to tell people what my film is about, but that whole process of finding a job—filling out applications, interviewing, having to sell yourself—is humiliating. I feel for those people. It comes through in Willie K's character. Now Merton has never worked, but he goes from boy to man in one week while trying to find a job."

Kohne grew up on Maui, where he attended Baldwin High School in Kahului and made Super 8 films. In college he worked in sports journalism, and later worked in television, film and even sales and marketing in Silicon Valley. Back on Maui, he produced the Barefoot Natives group. But making movies, Maui movies, was always the goal. "I'm very passionate about home and culture," he told me. "I want people who've learned these skills to come home and live here. Movies are the most powerful art form invented by man. And the indigenous movie industry here needs help. The way people can help is by supporting local filmmaking—even when the movie sucks. By doing so, you're helping us turn the corner and become better producers, better writers."

Which brings me to Kohne's next film, which was titled simply *Maui* when it began streaming, but it was released on Maui as *Kuleana*. While the film doesn't suck by any means, it was far more ambitious than *Get a Job,* and as a result isn't nearly as tightly focused. The film, which Kohne again wrote and directed (though he didn't edit it this time) tells the story of a Hawaiian family torn apart by an unscrupulous land developer. The film touches on the U.S.

Navy's use of the Island of Kahoʻolawe as a bombing range, organized crime, and the rebirth of Hawaiian culture in the 1970s. It's a gritty crime drama with a touch of magical realism, and Kohne made it with a tiny fraction of the budget that Hollywood epics typically draw. It's also a uniquely Hawaiian story, and includes actors who are actually from Hawaiʻi.

In 2016, I visited the set on one of the final production days. There I found Jim Oxborrow standing in his living room. Located in Waiehu, the house was decorated with nautical models, and framed deck plans of ocean liners like the *Titanic* and *Andrea Doria* hanging on the walls. Off to his left, two people were staring intently into laptop screens. Another was doing the same on his right. Ahead of him in the spacious kitchen, one woman was carefully weaving dark extensions into another woman's hair. As Oxborrow looked around the room, it was clear from his expression that it's all good.

These people, and many more, had been in and out of Oxborrow's house for four days. They were the cast and crew of *Kuleana*. I teasingly asked him if they've trashed the place, but he shook his head. "They've been so respectful it's amazing," he said. They even gave Oxborrow, an actor himself, a bit part.

Kohne worked on the *Kuleana* story for a decade or so. Set on Maui in both 1959 and 1971, the movie tells the story of two Hawaiians, Nohea and Kim, and how they deal with a powerful land developer named Victor Coyle. The movie touches on a variety of concepts and themes seldom seen in motion pictures. "For me, growing up on Maui—having been alive when they were bombing Kahoʻolawe—these things are still heavy on our conscience," Kainoa Horcajo, a Hawaiian cultural specialist who also has a small role in the movie ("Bill Kanekoa"), told me that day. "[The movie] is part of a larger societal discussion that we need to have on the future of Maui."

What's more, at a time when Hollywood routinely casts whites as "locals" (Emma Stone in *Aloha* was one of the more appalling examples), Kohne cast actors like Sonya Balmores and *True Blood*'s Kristina Anapau (she plays "Rose Coyle" in *Kuleana,* and is the executive producer) who are originally from Hawaiʻi.

Kohne originally anticipated shooting the movie in 2014, then distributing it to film festivals in 2015. That schedule didn't work out (because of that age-old friend/enemy of filmmakers: money), but by late spring of 2016, Kohne finally got to the point that he could make his film. After inviting me to visit the set, I stopped by Oxborrow's house—which the crew was using as a "base camp." After arriving at 10:00 a.m., Kathy Collins, a local actor and radio DJ who was working as an associate producer as well as location manager, met me outside. She quickly introduced me to actress Sonya Balmores, then left to get back to work.

While chatting with Balmores, makeup artist Judy Cunningham did the actress's hair. Balmores plays the adult version of "Kim"—"I can't pass for 10 anymore," she joked. She told me that she knew Stefan Schaefer, who is both *Kuleana*'s producer and one of its stars (he plays "Victor Coyle," the land developer). She previously appeared in the Bethany Hamilton biopic *Soul Surfer,* the TV series *Beyond the Break* and a 2014 episode of *Hawaii Five-0* (she played a tour bus robber). Balmores grew up in Kauaʻi, but was now living in Los Angeles.

"There aren't a lot of local Hawaiian stories," she told me as Cunningham weaved extensions into her hair. "I wanted to be part of that. Other films in Hawaiʻi may have a moke or an aunty in them, but here, my character speaks Hawaiian."

Though a full-length feature, Kohne opted for a tight shooting schedule—a mere 15 days. "I've never done a shooting schedule this tight," Director of Photography Dan Hersey told me. When I mentioned the schedule to Balmores, she simply smiled. "Sooo busy!" she said. "Every day for the last month. We finished at 11 last night. But when they offer you a job in Maui for a few months, it's hard to say no."

As we talked, it started to rain. The crew gathered around the living room began wondering aloud how it would affect the shoot, which was taking place just down the road. "Will they film in the pouring rain?" one crew member asked. The answer, of course, was yes. Though the crew had already shot scenes in Waiehu, Maʻalaea and other areas of Central Maui, rain was a new wrinkle they had to deal with. "Today's the first day it rained," Balmores said. "But that's what's fun about filming in Hawaiʻi—you cannot control the weather."

A few minutes later, makeup department head Natalie Bruce, production assistant Felippe De Souza and I got in a minivan and headed down the road to the actual set. Setting the movie in two distinct eras (there are also special effects requirements) poses a challenge for Bruce—1950s curls vs. more hippie hairstyles. Still, she was undaunted. "I can do any era of makeup," she said as De Souza slowly drove us down a dirt side road.

Known by the crew as "Grandma's House," the set was a grassy field beside a wooden house that dates to the 1930s. Trees ring the property, which sits above a tributary of the Waiehu Stream. It's a gorgeous piece of property, though not all of *Kuleana* takes place in such lush locations. A few hours after the shoot here ended, the crew caravanned back to Oxborrow's house to shoot a few scenes in a nearby jungle. There, decaying mangoes covered the ground, which made the air heavy with flies (bug repellant was plentiful).

But that was later. At Grandma's House, a dozen people were clustered around a bright red '57 Chevy Bel Air with a sign saying "Coyle Construction" on the door.

"The sign was originally much larger," Jack Grace, a local photographer who took all the movie stills for the production told me a little while after I arrived. "But it wouldn't stick to the bottom of the door, so they had to cut it down."

It's the third day the crew's been at this location. It's still drizzling, and the crew is huddled under umbrellas (at one point, I was surprised when a production assistant suddenly materialized at my side with an umbrella as I was scribbling in my notepad). The sky was gray, but the overall light was diffuse, an advantage to the crew. And the rain stopped a few minutes after I arrived.

There are people all over—prop assistants, lighting assistants, makeup designers, sound people. Everyone, it seemed, had a radio hookup. "It's highly regulated," Horcajo told me. "Everybody has their task—not to be cliché, everybody has their kuleana. And the more everyone does their job, everything goes smoothly."

The scene being shot was simple: Coyle (played by Schaefer) is leaning against the Chevy, reading a newspaper blaring the headline "STATEHOOD" when the younger versions of Nohea (played by 11-year-old Ryan Ursua) and Kim (11-year-old Kealani Warner, who was also a classmate of Ursua's) talk with him briefly. It's a straightforward scene, 30 seconds on the screen at most, but it was fraught with challenges—some typical to motion pictures, others unique to Maui filmmaking.

Kohne wanted a variety of angles in the scene, which took time. The scene called for Coyle to smoke, but because Schaefer's a non-smoker, he stood awkwardly with the cigarette between takes. Over and over, the actors—including the kids—repeated their one or two lines as the track-mounted camera filmed them from the front, behind, the side and afar. The scene also called for Ursua, who is carrying a rather sharp wooden spear, to thrust it through the newspaper Schaefer's reading. Grace, who stood next to me for some of the shoot, audibly winced as the spear punched through the prop paper towards Schaefer's face.

"We only have three prop newspapers," Production Designer Burt Sakata told me. "It was tough getting them printed." That meant the prop people had to prepare the papers carefully for each shot so the audience wouldn't see that they'd already been punctured. Keeping that—and myriad other details—straight from shot to shot is known as "continuity" in the movie business, and it's of supreme importance, especially in a film that jumps between two distinct historical time periods. Seeing a character suddenly wearing slippers when previously filmed with bare feet, or spying the VW bus in the background of a shot set in 1959, would immediately cause the audience to fail to "suspend disbelief," as movie people like to say, and propel them mentally out of the movie.

Keeping that from happening in *Kuleana* was the responsibility of Darren Corrao, the script supervisor. As Kohne moved between the cast and a video screen draped in a black sheet that allowed him to see what the camera was recording, and 1st Director Justin Hogan yelled "Quiet!" and "Action!" and made sure everyone was doing what they were supposed to be doing, Corrao stood a few yards away under a small shelter in front of a laptop that displayed both the visuals being filmed and a copy of the *Kuleana* script, turned to whatever scene was being filmed. On his shoulders rested responsibility for spotting continuity errors. At one point that morning, Corrao noticed that he could see a hole in the newspaper Schaefer was holding before Ursua had punctured it. When shooting shifted to a scene involving Balmores playing with a dog (Lucy, who was actually Oxborrow's dog), Corrao said the dog couldn't wear a collar because there was no collar in previous scenes. He also noticed that Schaefer did not pull a Polaroid camera out of the car at the end of the scene, even though earlier scenes included the camera. In fact, the camera was gone—an understandable oversight, given the tight shooting schedule, complex time period changes and the fact that *Kuleana* (like most movies) was shot out of chronological sequence.

To help, Corrao took many, many continuity shots with a smartphone, which allowed him to quickly check what an actor was wearing during previous shots. This helped immeasurably during one scene when Corrao noticed that the shirt worn by lead actor Moronai Kanekoa (who plays the elder "Nohea") didn't have enough sweat on it to match its appearance in two scenes shot a few days earlier. "So we had to spray the shirt," Corrao said.

When you have so many people working so closely for such long hours, accidents will happen. I was at the house just a few minutes before someone mentioned "the toupee incident" (I found no shortage of cast and crew members willing to corroborate the story). While filming a dramatic scene at Waiehu Stream, Schaefer ended up losing the toupee he'd been wearing in the water. Though crew members jumped in and tried to grab it, they were unsuccessful. Where the toupee ultimately ended up, no one could say, though Schaefer later told me that Kathy Collins brought in one of her wigs, which after trimming, worked just fine.

Schaefer moved to Maui seven years ago. He met Kohne in a way that, to use a cliché, is straight out of a movie: he answered a Craigslist want ad for a movie producer. The ad was for *Get A Job* (he had a small role in that movie as well). Many of the crew members worked on *Get A Job,* or for Schaefer when he produced movies in New York in the past, or both.

"We have a terribly ambitious shooting schedule," Schaefer told me when his scenes were wrapped up. "It's only working because we have so many people pitching in. Shooting seven to eight pages a day is aggressive in a studio setting. In the elements, it's lunacy. But we're pulling it off so far."

Between takes, Kohne joked to me about the rough schedule. "I'm lucky production's still talking to me," Kohne said. "It's just a really ambitious project. The shooting schedule is dictated by money."

Kohne refused to talk to me about the specifics of the movie's budget. In 2013, he had told me he could make *Kuleana* for $1 million. On the set itself, he would only say that his budget is less than that amount. This is hardly surprising, given Kohne's story—how do you pitch a movie in which the antagonist is an unscrupulous land developer to potential investors on Maui, most of whom have at least some financial interest in real estate?

In any case, Kohne insisted that having the full million wouldn't have made much difference. "I can't say that we would have made a better movie," he said. "I don't know how anyone could've done what we've done here. It's the result of the commitment and passion of so many." Still, Kohne said it's better than his experience on *Get A Job*. "This time, I knew what to shoot, and what not to," he said.

As everyone wrapped up the shoot at Grandma's House, Kohne thanked the property owner for the use of the place.

"So when I can go to the mall and see the movie?" he asked.

Kohne hesitated. "Not sure it's going to be at the mall," Kohne said. "We're going to focus on international festivals first."

Given all that Kohne has taken on himself, it's remarkable he's made it this far. Not only has he made a motion picture, but he's nearly finished with a second one in a completely different genre—all filmed on Maui. This isn't a big studio flying an expensive, big-name cast to the islands for a few exterior shots, then doing the rest in Southern California sound stages. What Kohne did transcends merely making a movie on Maui—he set out to make a Maui movie industry. One dedicated to letting Maui people tell Maui stories. It's been difficult and expensive, and though Kohne said he has been able to use Hawai'i tax credits for local film productions, the rest of the work and support comes from himself and his crew.

"It's a real leap of faith," Kohne told me. "This is not for the timid. But if *Kuleana* inspires one filmmaker or one writer to take a leap, then we've achieved our goal."

Whether he did that, though, remains to be seen. Though both *Get a Job* and *Kuleana* (*Maui*) won film festival awards, neither is streaming anywhere today, which means the only way to see them is to purchase DVDs.

CHAPTER 25

LAHAINA AND PARADISE

Nothing about the Lahaina wildfire surprised me. Not the scale, the destruction or even the death toll, which, to be perfectly honest, I thought would be much higher given the haphazard (at best) evacuation of the town. County officials didn't even blow the emergency warning sirens even though they are part of an all-hazard alert system that includes wildfires, and in the days immediately after the blaze, when a Google document with thousands of names of missing people began to get circulated, I feared the number of dead would be astronomical.

Thirteen days after the August 8 fire, President Joe Biden visited Lahaina. With his wife, Jill, he walked down Front Street, and saw block after block of devastation, then he spoke under the old Banyan Tree (which arborists at the time said was badly burned, but still alive) about his efforts to expedite federal assistance to disaster survivors. With him were a gaggle of federal, state and local officials. One of them, Senator Mazie Hirono, spoke of what she experienced that day a couple weeks later on the floor of the U.S. Senate. Her description of what was left of the town, and its residents, deserves to be quoted at length:

> Front Street, once vibrant with the sounds of music and revelers in the air, is now eerily quiet—the only sound to be heard is often the clanging of twisted metal in the wind. At the hotels where survivors are staying, I met parents afraid to send their children to school, not wanting them out of their sight. I met a woman who escaped the fire with just a backpack of belongings—a backpack she now takes everywhere with her, refusing to take it off her back. And I met hotel workers and others, especially a health worker who said that, weeks after the fires, some residents and workers were so traumatized, they didn't even want to come out of their rooms.

Nearly 8,000 people lived in Lahaina on the morning of August 8, 2023. It's a good bet the vast majority, if not all, of the survivors are traumatized. Everyone lost something—a home, family possessions, pet, car, business, job, loved ones. Many lost all of that. A sense of dread settled over the entire island. "There was just this super unsettling depression hanging in most places," my friend and former *MauiTime* colleague Sarah Gerlach told me in October. She said it was everywhere—stores, gas stations, even places far from Lahaina. "Nobody seems to be doing well, even if their employment and income are still super solid," she said. "There is just this underlying sense of unease and fear for the unknown future."

And this was after West Maui officially reopened to tourists. But why people would choose to visit, even stay, in a place so close to unimaginable death and destruction concerned residents long before Governor Green announced the reopening of West Maui hotels. State officials had already said in September that airline surveys showed many visitors were canceling their Maui vacations, or at least postponing them, out of a feeling of "guilt." Those who presumably didn't feel bad about staying in hotels staffed by people who were likely still grieving and suffering were either merely clueless or prompted by something more nefarious.

"You'd hope that wouldn't be necessary, but disaster and dark tourism has been a real thing since Mt. Vesuvius erupted in Pompeii in, like, 79 AD," resident Jen Mather told the Maui County Council during its September 1 meeting on a proposal to spend money earmarked for tourism management on marketing. "It's never gone away and it never will."

Dark tourism is "the act of travel to sites of death, disaster or places associated with the seemingly macabre," according to Professor Philip R. Stone, director of the Institute for Dark Tourism Research at the University of Central Lancashire. Stone has studied dark tourism extensively, and told me that people who seek out grim experiences will likely find Lahaina a desirable place to visit.

Over the past two decades, there has been a growing interest "in selectively recalling our troubled pasts, thereby offering contemporary tourists to sightsee in the mansions of the dead," Stone said. "Lahaina has lost its beauty and, as a result of the fires, has become a place arrested in time and place. It is the extraordinary against the ordinary that many people find interest in, and the 'tourist gaze' will undoubtedly find Lahaina 'attractive' in its deathly landscape." Maui, for lack of a better phrase, is a mess right now—physically, financially, emotionally. Visiting Maui (or anywhere in Hawai'i, really) has always been difficult for the thoughtful traveler, but now, the price is beyond stratospheric. "There is a fine, blurred line between commemoration and commercialism, and tourists need emotional intelligence to respect that line," Stone said.

Of course, exactly how many Lahaina residents will stay to defend the land against disaster selfies is still very much an open question. Foster Ampong, the Hawaiian activist who was so vocal about the old Pioneer Mill two decades ago, hasn't been shy about telling the Maui County Council about his myriad family members who left the island shortly after the fire—there was simply no room to house them with family outside West Maui, and they had no desire to live in temporary shelters. "They want to come home," he told the council in late August, imploring them to take the post-fire diaspora into account when planning for West Maui's recovery.

* * *

Lahaina will recover. Lahaina will rebuild. But ensuring Lahaina will be resilient to future wildfire danger requires the county to repair its "broken" relationship with the land, more than one wildfire expert testified in the weeks following the blaze.

Warning Maui of the dangers of wildfires is nothing new to Elizabeth Pickett. Since 2008, Pickett has researched the risk towns on Maui faced from such fires for the Hawai'i Wildfire Management Organization, a Hawai'i Island–based nonprofit set up specifically to analyze and publicize the dangers facing the state. In 2014, four years before a wildfire nearly destroyed Lahaina and nine years prior to the wildfire that did, Pickett co-wrote a stunning report titled Western Maui Community Wildfire Protection Plan. Running well over 100 pages, the report laid out in detail the "extreme" risk wildfires posed not just to Lahaina, but South and Central Maui as well. Though the report and its recommendations were highlighted in the West Maui Community Plan—a core planning document adopted by the Maui County Council in 2021—nothing substantial was carried out prior to August 8, 2023.

The reason for all of it was clear: the "unmanaged land" that used to be fields of cane but was now vast tracts of invasive, highly flammable grasses that now surrounded Lahaina, Kīhei and even the Central Maui plains. And with each successive fire, burned native vegetation often gave way to even more flammable non-native grasses, according to Pickett. This process dates back to the mid-nineteenth century, when streams that originally fed places like Lahaina were diverted for sugar crop production, according to Dr. Clay Trauernicht, an ecosystems and fire specialist from the University of Hawai'i at Mānoa. With those sugar lands now fallow and covered with unmanaged, often extremely flammable grasses, the total area that has burned in Hawai'i over the last three decades has risen by 300 percent, Trauernicht told a Maui County Council committee in mid-September.

The August 8 Lahaina fire exemplified the entire county's "broken" relationship with the land, Trauernicht told the councilmembers. For that reason, Maui needs an "island-wide vegetation management plan," Pickett said. "Land, water and equity issues are at the heart of this," she added. But simply planting native vegetation wouldn't necessarily solve the problem. Former cane fields didn't just burn in wildfires because they were greener, but because the land was regularly managed then, Trauernicht emphasized.

The county, state, somebody, had to manage the land around Maui's towns, both fire prevention experts testified, or what happened in Lahaina on August 8 would happen again. Proper land management would help produce "thriving landscapes" that don't expose nearby communities to wildfires, Pickett said. But that also requires a vastly strengthened regulatory regime, where the owners of vast tracts of land covered in flammable grasses face rigorous enforcement, according to Pickett.

Of course, all of this requires more funding, Pickett said. Funding, she said, has been all but nonexistent in the last decade. "This is what's broken my heart," Pickett told the councilmembers.

* * *

Three days after the Lahaina wildfire, I called Greg Bolin. Few people anywhere in the world knew not only what Lahaina residents were going through, but what lay in store for them. Bolin, the current mayor of Paradise, California, was there in November 2018 when a wildfire overwhelmed his town, killing 85 residents and destroying about 12,000 homes. He said he and other Paradise residents have been watching news reports on the Lahaina fire with great concern, and familiarity.

Nearly five years later, the town is still rebuilding, and is nowhere near what it once was. It probably never will be. Once housing about 26,000 residents, today the population of Paradise is just a little over 9,000, according to Bolin. Many people, too exhausted, saddened and scared to go through the hardship of trying to stay and rebuild, simply left. "I lost a ton of friends," Bolin said of people who decided to leave Paradise after the fire. Though he never considered leaving the town he'd lived in since he was nine years old, Bolin did wonder at times how it would be possible to save the town. "I did not want to give in and move," he said. "It wasn't a question of bringing Paradise back, but were we capable of pulling this off?"

To help convince people to stay, Bolin said the town council agreed to 41 goals demanded by residents. Those included installing warning sirens—which is expected to be complete next month—and getting rid of dead-end roads, which had trapped many of the people who died while trying to escape.

But rebuilding has been slow. So far, Paradise has rebuilt just over 2,000 homes, but it wasn't until last year that the town began rebuilding its roads. "They take a beating with cars melting on them," he said of the damage. According to Bolin, these new roadways are expected to be complete around 2026, nearly eight years after the fire. Another key factor to bringing life back to Paradise was rebuilding churches and schools. "FEMA told us to get schools and churches back," Bolin said. "If you can't do that, they said, forget it."

Bolin recalled the town's schools reopened very soon after the fire, operating out of warehouses in nearby Chico. He also said the town, what was left of it, rallied around the high school football team. "They missed their playoff game that year because of the fire," he said. "But the next year, they came back. One kid, his parents moved to San Diego but he stayed in Chico with his aunt because he wanted to play football in Paradise. That brought the town together." As for churches, Bolin said one of the largest in town was saved from burning in the fire by an alert maintenance worker who managed to cut down enough trees around the building to keep it intact. Big enough to hold 2,000 people, it was where the town council met after the fire. Other churches in town weren't so fortunate, and are only now getting rebuilt.

The town's hospital closed, Bolin said, adding that just a week before I called, officials announced that it wouldn't reopen. Today, the closest hospital to Paradise residents is 30 minutes away.

What happened in Paradise won't necessarily translate directly to Lahaina, but there's no question that starting to rebuild won't happen anytime soon. In the meantime, Bolin said the most important thing for residents is to rest. "You have to find a way to rest," he said. "It's difficult but you have to." He said community groups were key to Paradise's recovery. Soon after the fire, they organized free dinners for residents to meet and talk. "We did that for two, three years," Bolin said. "People need to get together and talk. And they should cry when they need to cry."

Bolin said it was months before he and others in town really laughed again. A big help came at one of those community dinners, when residents went around the table telling everyone the things they hurriedly grabbed when they evacuated their homes after the fire broke out. "It was some of the funniest things you heard," Bolin said. "One woman said she grabbed a plate of deviled eggs. We busted up. People need to laugh."

People will also be angry. Emotions will be raw, Bolin said. This is understandable. The old camaraderie can come back, he said, but it will take determination. In October, Lahaina residents finally got the okay to return to what was left of their homes. Doing so is absolutely necessary, but it will bring all the pain back, Bolin said.

"It will be tough to go through your things," he added. "But you will find stuff that made it, and you will cherish those things."

EPILOGUE

In late August, 2023, I got in my car and drove about 10 minutes north on the 405 freeway. There, in Carson—a small suburb of Los Angeles—I parked next to a cramped beige restaurant. Called Back Home in Lahaina, the place is a time capsule, decorated inside in eerie detail to resemble Lahaina in the late 1990s, which is when the restaurant first opened. Bright colors—baby blue, bright red, emerald green—welcomed me when I walked in. Fake storefronts evoking shops along Front Street lined the hallway between the to-go counter and the dining room. I was seated near a giant painting of the old *Carthaginian* sailing ship at sunset, which stood near a facade of the old Pioneer Inn, which stood near the waterfront for over a century. Waiting for my chicken katsu plate lunch, I must have spent 10 minutes staring at a beige wall panel next to a giant mural of Front Street that was meant to evoke the Marketplace at Lahaina, a small gathering of shops and restaurants I'd visited countless times during my lunch breaks. On my way out, I noticed a facade of the little Lahaina train station, a tiny tourist attraction on the north end of town where you could ride the famed "Sugar Cane Train" up to Kāʻanapali and back.

It was a surreal experience, sure, but I also felt immediately comfortable there. I wasn't alone in that, either. In the days and weeks after the fire, members of the Maui diaspora, or just people with family members still living there, would gather at Back Home. The restaurant became a "beacon of hope" for people connected to Hawaiʻi to "congregate, mourn and celebrate over live music and heaping plates of rice and macaroni salad, slabs of sweet short ribs and piles of crispy fried chicken," Lucas Quan Peterson wrote in the *Los Angeles Times* a week after the fire.

And there are a lot of people connected to Hawaiʻi in Southern California. In fact, there are apparently more Native Hawaiians and Pacific Islanders in California than in Hawaiʻi itself. That's according to the authors of *Hawaiians in Los Angeles,* one of those slim books with a sepia-toned cover that's often sold in museums. The reason for the diaspora is a complex mix of economics, the post-contact decimation of the Hawaiian population and what the authors call the "slippery" definition of what "Hawaiian" ethnicity actually means. The popularity of Southern California itself is probably owed a lot to climate as well as the military–industrial complex that connects the region to both Hawaiʻi and the Pacific itself. The result of all this can be seen everywhere in Southern California, if you know what to look for. L&L Hawaiian Barbecue restaurants are, while not exactly ubiquitous, certainly popular.

Hawaiian culture is especially popular in places like Huntington Beach, where a statue of the famed Hawaiian surfer and swimmer Duke Kahanamoku looks across Pacific Coast Highway and Hawaiian festivals, complete with local hālau hula, occasionally take place across the street at the Huntington Pier. A few blocks from the water is the Huntington Beach International Surf Museum, a tiny but vibrant building holding a host of Hawaiʻi surf memorabilia, including a few displays dedicated to both Duke and Eddie Aikau, the latter of which included a portion of a lifeguard tower covered in handwritten dedications to Aikau from major surfers.

All of this had become known to me prior to the August 8 fire, but after the blaze I realized I'd never left Maui. The island was, and remains, all around me. It will be even if I leave Southern California. This is not because Maui holds some special magic, or that it touched my soul in some divine way. Maui is the only place I ever lived that forced me to think about my place in society— the value of the work I did, and the scale of the harm I could cause. Maui tells everyone who visits these lessons, but not everyone listens. A person like Kent Smith ("Growth is inevitable. Growth is inevitable. . . .") lived there decades longer than I ever did, and he never listened. It didn't happen overnight with me, but eventually I did listen. And when I did, Maui became a home for me, even if I never set foot on the island again.

Index

Aikau, Eddie (Aikau, Edward Ryan Makua Hanai), 78–81, 127, 144
Akaka, Abraham, 31, 83
Akaka, Daniel, 17, 24
Akimseu, Momi, 100
Alboro, Fuzzy Sr., 47
Alcubilla, Sergio, 3
Altemus-Williams, Imani, 73
Ampong, Foster, 49, 139
Anapau, Kristina, 131
Andaya, Herman, 117
Andrews, Lorrin, 83
Antone, Rod, 86, 122
Arakawa, Alan, 67, 92, 94, 98

Baldwin, James, 72
Balmores, Sonya, 131, 132
Balraj, Sumithra, 65
Beppu, Tadao, 107
Biden, Joe, 4, 33, 137
Blackburn-Rodriguez, Tom, 44
Blackford, Mansel, 109
Bolin, Greg, 140
Borge, Christine, 4
Brown, Gordon, 53

Caldito, Richard, 108
Camara, Jason, 39
Carrao, Darren, 134
Chinery, Tran, 94
Ching, David, 84–88
Choy, Frederick, 57
Chun, Malcolm Nāea, 82, 83
Cleveland, Glover, 16
Clinton, Bill, 17
Collins, Kathy, 131, 135
Coloma, Lydia, 3
Coolidge, Jennifer 126
Cooper, Jim, 67

Corwin, Adriane Raff, 103
Couch, Don, 99
Cowles, Barbara, 125
Cowles, Joseph, 125
Cravalho, Elmer, 107
Crosthwaite, Eugene, 60

Davenport, Kiana, 22–25
Davis, Chelsea, 2
De Souza, Felippe, 132
Domingo, Donna, 91
Donegan, Moira, 72
Draper, Randy, 64–68
Duncombe, Betsy, 35–40

Fleetwood, Mick, 129
Fortenberry, Ken, 56, 57, 60
Freeland, George "Keoki", 50

George, Sam, 79
Gerlach, Sarah, 138
Gilliom, Eric, 129
Grace, Jack, 133
Green, Josh, 4, 5
Grimes, Rick, 26
Guzman, Don, 68

Hamilton, Bethany, 132
Hanohano, Alexa, 1
Hara, Kenneth, 121
Hardman, Gilbert, 107
Herken, Gregg, 54, 56, 60
Hewahewa, Koa, 5, 6
Hill, David A., 57
Hirano, James, 38
Hirono, Mazie, 33
Hobro, Marie Eriel, 73
hooks, bell, 72
Horcajo, Kainoa, 131, 133
Houlgate, Deke, 57, 58

Iaukea, Curtis, 82
Ice, Phil, 61
Ige, David, 34, 90, 98, 120, 121
Ing, Kaniela, 20
Iaukea, Sydney, 10, 12, 19, 30, 31, 82, 88, 89

Jabola-Carolus, Khara, 72
Janion, Aubrey, 11
Johnson, Dwayne "The Rock", 20, 21
Joiner, Buck, 98–100
Jones, Robert Trent, 63
Justice, Daniel Heath, 72

K, Willie (Willie Kahaiali'i), 129, 130
Kaba, Mariame, 17
Kahanamoku, Duke, 79, 144
Kalākaua, 16, 46
Kaleikoa, Ka'eo, 72, 114–117
Kalepa, Archie, 78
Kamehameha III, 16
Kanekoa, Moronai, 134
Kaplan, Fred, 123
Keller, Ann, 41, 44
Kelly, Anna Keala, 21
Kennedy, John, 123
King, Kelly, 68
Kirch, Patrick Vinton, 14
Kobayashi, Blaine, 114, 115
Kohne, Brian, 129
Kuamo'o, Calvin, 26–29
Kuga, Mitchell, 127
Kukahiko, John, 108

Lansford, Kekoa, 1
Lili'uokalani, 16–18, 83, 114
Lyman-Mersereau, Marion, 81

Mailhot, Terese, 72
Manne, Kate, 72
Manuel, Kaleo, 116
Matin, Sharyn, 76
Mattis, James, 123
Mayer, Dick, 101, 106, 108
McCartney, Mike, 34, 98
McClung, David, 107
McKay, Jim, 79
McKinley, William, 16

McLean, Michele (McLean, Michele Chouteau), 10, 65–67
McLennan, Carol, 46, 91, 92
Mead, Clancy, 56, 60
Mellin, Tom, 97
Metcalfe, Simon, 11
Miyagi, Vern, 120
Molina, Mike, 97
Moriwake, Isaac, 93
Mossman, Ipo, 84–88
Murakami, Alan, 93
Murray, Jeffrey, 117, 118

Naeole, Clifford, 11, 12
Nelson, Willie, 129
Ness, Autumn, 3
Nishiki, Kai, 68
Nishiki, Wayne, 68
Nohara, Wes, 73
Nouchi, Alan, 38, 41

Oxborrow, Jim, 131, 132, 134

Pahukoa, Mary Ann, 20
Pai, Ajit, 119
Payne, William Harrison, 60
Peralta, Stacy, 79
Perez, Albert, 4, 86, 88, 101–104, 115
Peterson, Lucas Quan, 143
Pickett, Elizabeth, 139, 140
Pignataro, Frank, Jr., 53
Pignataro, Frank, Sr., 51, 53
Pignataro, Gus, 54
Pignataro, Marie, 53
Pignataro, Pasquale, 53
Pinataro, Albert F., 52–54
Pinataro, Jean, 51, 53

Rankine, Claudia, 72
Rasmussen, Teena, 99
Rodrigues, Louis, 57
Russo, Tommy, 71, 76

Saiki, Scott, 119
Schaefer, Stefan, 132–135
Schatz, Brian, 34, 90
Shane, Charlotte, 72

Slater, Kelly, 80
Smith, Kent, 10, 11, 102, 144
Solnit, Rebecca, 72
Sproat, Kapua, 20
Sugimura, Yuki Lei, 68
Swanson, David, 15
Szigeti, George, 121

Taublieb, Paul, 79
Tavares, Hannibal, 108
Tokioka, James, 4
Tomita, Les, 5
Tower, Wells, 73
Traister, Rebecca, 72
Trask, Haunani Kay, 31
Trask, Mililani, 31
Trauernicht, Clay, 139, 140
Trump, Donald, 25, 122
Tsutsui, Shan, 91

Vencyl, Terryl, 97, 98, 100, 101
Victorino, Mike, 96
Victorino, Shane, 96

Wakida, Clyde, 1, 2, 81
Wakida, Shigeto "Shigesh", 1
Warner, Kealani, 133
Webb, Casey, 5
West, Steven, 2
White, Curtis, 130
White, Mike (politician), 66, 68, 99
White, Mike (writer, director, actor), 125–128
Whitehead, Jim, 10
Wilcox, Allen C., Jr., 107
Wong-Kim, Evaon, 37, 38
Wriston, James III, 47

Zuckerberg, Mark, 20

About the Author

ANTHONY PIGNATARO is a journalist and author. A journalist since 1996, he spent 12 years as Editor of *MauiTime*, the last alternative newsweekly in Hawai'i, which sadly closed in late 2023. In addition, he has written for a variety of publications, some of which are still in print: *OC Weekly, Honolulu Weekly, Sacramento News & Review, Los Angeles* magazine*, East Bay* magazine, and *Long Beach Post*. He is the author of three novels, all set on Maui, and two one-act plays, both of which won awards at the Maui Fringe Festival and the PlayBuilders of Hawai'i Play Festival. He lives in Long Beach, California.